The Thriving Practice

Your Complete Blueprint for Building a Successful Private Practice in Mental Health

Dr. Daniela Rizzo, M.D.

Published by Rizzo Health Press

www.thethrivingpracticebookmd.com

This book is intended for educational and informational purposes only. It does not constitute legal, financial, medical, or other professional advice. The strategies and frameworks presented are based on the author's professional and clinical experience and may not apply to every situation. Laws, regulations, and professional standards vary by jurisdiction and are subject to change. Readers are strongly encouraged to consult qualified legal, financial, and healthcare professionals regarding their specific circumstances. The author and publisher disclaim any liability arising from the use or application of the information contained in this book.

The Thriving Practice: Your Complete Blueprint for Building a Successful Private Practice in Mental Health

First Edition

ISBN: 979-8-9954179-0-3

Dedication

For every doctor, psychologist, social worker, nurse practitioner, and mental health care provider who ever doubted they could make it—You can. And you will.

For my husband, James Rizzo—My support, love of my life, and best friend.

Epigraph

"Dr. Rizzo understands that success in mental health is not just about treating others - It's about creating a life and a practice that sustains the healer as well. Whether you are just beginning your practice or reimaging it after burnout, this book will meet you where you are and move you forward

— Jacob M. Appel, MD MS,MPH, Mount Sinai School of Medicine

Preface

This is the book I wish I had years ago, late at night, burned out, sitting at my desk after seeing too many patients, with tabs open on my computer that all read the same thing: "How to start a private practice."

Back then, I wasn't looking for theory or motivational slogans. I wanted something real. Something step-by-step. Something that would tell me: Yes, it's possible. Here's how. But what I found instead were scattered blogs, vague advice, and assumptions that I had a team of consultants or a trust fund behind me. I didn't. Maybe you don't either.

This book is for every clinician who has felt trapped in broken systems, undervalued by rigid structures, or unsure how to begin building something of their own. You're not alone, and you don't have to stay stuck. This is your blueprint. It doesn't require privilege, connections, or an MBA—only courage, clarity, and commitment.

Inside these pages, you'll find:

Actionable strategies, not fluff.

Checklists and scripts, not just concepts.

Real-world guidance drawn from lived experience, not theory from the sidelines.

Whether you're a psychiatrist, therapist, psychologist, or mental health provider at any stage—just imagining your first intake form or managing a full caseload and wondering how to scale—this book will meet you where you are. It's designed to reduce overwhelm and replace it with a confident, clear path forward.

You'll learn how to set up your practice legally, ethically, and profitably. You'll discover how to build a brand, attract clients who value your work, and lead your business with integrity and intention. But more than that, you'll be reminded that it is not selfish to want sustainability. That you are allowed to thrive while helping others heal. That financial empowerment and clinical excellence can, and must, coexist.

This book was written to be a companion on quiet nights, on early mornings, and during the pivotal moments when you wonder if you're really cut out for this. You are. The fact that you're holding this book tells me everything I need to know about your readiness.

So, take a deep breath. You don't have to figure it all out today. You just have to begin.

Here's to the healers who dare to lead. Let's build your thriving practice. Let's get to work.

—Dr. Daniela Rizzo, M.D.

Foreword

In medicine and literature, the greatest tools we have are stories and systems. What Dr. Daniela Rizzo has accomplished in *The Thriving Practice* is to provide both. With unflinching honesty and surgical clarity, she offers more than advice; she offers a path.

As someone who has spent decades at the intersection of ethics, psychiatry, and public discourse, I've seen countless clinicians struggle with the transition from training to independence. Many remain excellent practitioners, but too few become builders of systems, leaders of vision, or protectors of their own well-being. This book is the antidote.

Dr. Rizzo understands that success in mental health is not just about treating others; it's about creating a life and a practice that sustains the healer as well. She offers tools that are wise, accessible, and grounded in experience. Whether you are just beginning your practice or reimagining it after burnout, this book will meet you where you are and move you forward.

Dr. Rizzo has written a much-needed blueprint for mental health professionals who want more than survival—they want sovereignty. *The Thriving Practice* is a masterclass in transforming clinical skills into meaningful entrepreneurship. With practical insight, heartfelt honesty, and a visionary's courage, Dr. Rizzo empowers readers to build practices that heal both patients and providers. A must-read for every therapist, psychiatrist, and healer ready to take the reins.

—Jacob M. Appel, MD, JD, MPhil, Author of *Who Says You're Dead?* and *Phoning Home*, Mount Sinai School of Medicine, Bioethics & Psychiatry.

Table of Contents

Introduction

Welcome to the beginning of your journey toward professional independence and personal fulfillment. In a healthcare landscape often defined by bureaucracy, rigid structures, and overwhelming demand, *The Thriving Practice* serves as the essential roadmap that medical and clinical training often fails to provide. This book is not just a guide to business; it is a call to action for the healer who believes that meaningful clinical work and financial freedom can and must coexist.

The transition from a "worker" mindset, conditioned by years of hierarchical training, to an "owner" identity is the most significant shift you will make. This book facilitates that transformation by offering a step-by-step blueprint designed to replace overwhelm with a confident, clear path forward. You will be guided through the Private Practice Success Pyramid, a foundational framework consisting of three critical layers:

- Purpose: The bedrock of your practice, ensuring your work aligns with your deepest values and clinical mission.
- Structure: The operational backbone, covering the legal, financial, and systemic essentials required to run a smooth, HIPAA-compliant business.
- Visibility: The pinnacle that ensures those who need your expertise can find you through authentic branding and strategic outreach.

Whether you are a psychiatrist, psychologist, social worker, or nurse practitioner, the strategies within these pages are grounded in lived experience rather than abstract theory. This book provides the actionable tools, from scripts and checklists to financial formulas, necessary to build a practice that does not just survive, but thrives.

Ultimately, this book is about sovereignty. It is about designing a professional life that reflects who you are, protects your well-being, and allows you to create a lasting legacy of healing. You have already mastered the art of medicine and therapy; now, it is time to master the art of leading your own vision. Your thriving practice begins here.

Chapter 1: The Proven Path to Private Practice Success

"Wherever the art of medicine is loved, there is also a love of humanity." – Hippocrates

When you graduate from medical school, no one hands you a blueprint for success in private practice. You're given a degree, but the roadmap to freedom? That's something you must create yourself.

Throughout your training, you've been equipped to save lives, diagnose with precision, and manage crises others can't handle. But what you haven't been taught—what very few of us are taught—is how to build a life and career rooted in freedom, alignment, and autonomy. How to step beyond hospital walls, break free from institutional structures, and say with conviction: "This is mine. I lead this."

It's often at this moment, right at the edge of desire and doubt, that many clinicians hesitate, unsure of what comes next. But hesitation doesn't change the reality around us.

The mental health crisis in America isn't just a headline; it's reality. According to the National Alliance on Mental Illness, one in five adults experiences mental illness each year. Yet many are left waiting weeks, sometimes months, for an appointment. This gap between need and access presents a powerful opportunity. The healthcare system may be overwhelmed, but you have a chance to step outside it and offer solutions on your own terms.

Let's not kid ourselves; the healthcare system is broken. Bureaucracy, red tape, and rigid limitations define the old ways. You were trained to be a healer, but the question is: are you ready to become a leader?

This shift from clinician to leader isn't about abandoning your training; it's about expanding your purpose. The landscape of healthcare is shifting faster than ever. Telemedicine has erased geographic boundaries, allowing you to reach people once out of reach. Direct-pay models are rising as patients rebel against insurance-driven systems, seeking personalized care that aligns with their needs. And as stigma around mental health fades, the demand for services grows rapidly.

This is a perfect storm of opportunity for the entrepreneurial clinician. It's not a matter of if you can succeed; it's a matter of when you decide to seize it. And the best part? You already have everything you need to begin. This chapter is your compass—not because it outlines every step (every journey is unique), but because it reminds you that you already hold the map. You don't need anyone's permission to step into your power. The world is waiting for what you have to offer. You are not behind. You are exactly where you need to be.

I didn't grow up with business mentors or MBA programs. What I had was urgent necessity. I came from poverty—at 14, I was living on the streets of Los Angeles before moving to Brazil with nothing but my grandparents' support. I learned Portuguese while completing high school and medical school simultaneously, studying 10-hour days, crying from exhaustion but refusing to quit.

After medical school, I worked across specialties in rural Brazil—emergency medicine, surgery, family practice, even delivering babies in hospitals with 150 patients waiting daily. One memory crystallized why I do this work: a young boy fell from a roof while flying his kite. Despite the crushing patient load, I rushed him through, coordinated with neurosurgery, and saved his life. Six months later, his father found me: "He's playing soccer now." That's why we do this.

But burnout was real. I returned to the US in my 30s with no safety net—working as a waitress and teacher while volunteering in neurosurgery departments and shadowing specialists. My USMLE scores weren't perfect, but my mission was bigger than any obstacle. I passed what I needed for residency, built my credentials step by step, and eventually Googled "how to start a private practice" during ER shifts while burned out and exhausted.

I didn't have capital, connections, or a blueprint. What I had was lived experience in broken systems and a vision for something better. That's what this book delivers—not theory, but the step-by-step path I walked so you don't have to figure it out alone.

You are not the first to face this crossroads, and you won't be the last; you are not alone in this. Others have walked this path, too. Many people have walked away from jobs that no longer served them—jobs that drained their energy and stifled their potential. Take Dr. Sarah, a well-established therapist working in a hospital system. She was seeing 10 to 12 clients a day, feeling burnt out, overwhelmed, and emotionally exhausted. The red tape and pressure to meet quotas left little room for self-care or meaningful connection. She realized that to better care for her patients and herself, she had to leave the system and start a private practice. Now, Dr. Sarah has the freedom to build a practice that reflects her values and fosters deeper, more meaningful client relationships.

Then there's Dr. Mark, a psychiatrist who spent years in a busy outpatient clinic, seeing patients for just fifteen minutes at a time and burning the candle at both ends. The constant pressure to meet quotas left him emotionally drained, with no time for reflection or rest. His turning point came when he realized he was losing the very passion that had drawn him to medicine. Today, he runs a private practice where he can offer longer sessions, charge what he's worth, and, most importantly, rediscover the joy and purpose in his work.

These stories illustrate something crucial. I'm sharing them because burnout isn't an abstract concept; it's real, and it's painful. But you don't have to stay trapped in that cycle. You can build a life and career that sustains you and nourishes your soul. It doesn't matter if you've been stuck for years or if your dream feels out of reach. I promise, with purpose and action, change is within your grasp.

Here's what I realized along my journey: the only difference between where I was and where I wanted to be was action. And the only thing standing between you and the life you want? It's the same—action.

I understand the fear, uncertainty, and self-doubt that might be holding you back. Believe me, I've been there. I know what it's like to question whether you're ready or if you're enough. But here's the truth: the very fact that you're reading this book, that you're willing to take action and do things differently, speaks volumes.

Similarly, there are countless mental health providers who've overcome burnout and built thriving practices. Dr. Nancy, a psychologist who burned out after years in a high-pressure environment, finally took the leap into private practice. Not only did she rediscover her passion, but she also created a business that prioritized both her well-being and the needs of her clients.

Dr. James, a psychiatrist who had burned out in the public healthcare system, started a private practice that allowed him to set his own schedule, focus on quality care, and fall back in love with his work.

These stories aren't unique; they reflect what's possible when you take control of your future. This is where inspiration gives way to application. Now it's your turn.

You don't have to wait for the stars to align or for the perfect moment to arrive; that moment is right now. You don't need more credentials or outside validation. What you need is belief—belief in yourself and the courage to step into your power. The road ahead may not be easy, but it's one you can walk. And the rewards will reach far beyond what you can imagine today.

Here's the best part: you are not alone. Just as I had to find my way, so will you—but this time, your path will be clearer, your steps more intentional, your actions supported by the structure you need to succeed. That purpose leads directly to why this book exists. This book is your guide—a step-by-step blueprint to help you build your practice from the ground up.

But where do you start? The truth is, no one handed me a manual on how to do it. I didn't have someone showing me the ropes or guiding me through each challenge. I had to figure it out myself, and so will you. What makes the difference, however, is not perfection—it's mindset.

But what you need (and what I needed) is the mindset to keep going, even when the road feels hard. What you need is the unshakable belief that you have what it takes to build something extraordinary.

Like the entrepreneurs before you, you can build a business that doesn't just survive—it thrives. Yes, it will challenge you. It will test you. But when you look back, you'll see how far you've come—the fears you've overcome, the wins you've earned, the clarity you've built. And you'll know, without a doubt, that you didn't just build a practice; you built a legacy.

Remember: Clarity fuels momentum, and momentum leads to mastery. Without clarity, it's easy to feel lost or overwhelmed. You can get bogged down in technical details and logistics, never fully understanding the deeper why behind what you're doing. But once you choose to move forward with clarity, everything changes.

Here's why:

- Clarity gives you direction. You know exactly what you're working toward. You're not just checking tasks off a list; you're building something with intention.

- Clarity fuels your focus. Without a clear vision, it's easy to get distracted by every new trend or shiny object. But when your *why* is clear, your focus sharpens, and distractions lose their power.
- Clarity makes difficult decisions easier. The road to starting your practice won't always be smooth. You will face challenges. But your ability to make confident decisions depends on how clear you are about your purpose.

Now that we've established the role clarity plays, it's also important to understand what this book will and will not do. Let's be clear about what this book won't do for you:

- It won't feed you fluff or empty affirmations. This isn't about quick-fix motivation. This book is for action takers—people ready to take real steps toward their goals.
- It won't drown you in jargon or unnecessary tech. This isn't about making things harder than they have to be. You don't need to be a tech expert or business strategist to build your practice. The steps here are clear, simple, and actionable.
- It won't assume you have unlimited resources. I know you might be starting with limited capital, few connections, or very little time. This book meets you where you are, offering practical, realistic steps no matter your starting point.

Now, let's shift into what this book will help you build.

- It will give you the tools, clarity, and confidence to launch your private practice.
- Step-by-step guidance: Every strategy and piece of advice comes from real-world experience. I've walked this path, and I'll show you how to take your first steps, even if you're short on time and juggling a busy schedule.
- Help you shed fear: Fear is a natural part of the process. This book will show you how to use that fear as fuel for momentum instead of letting it hold you back.
- Overcome scarcity and comparison: It's easy to look at others who seem "further ahead." This book will help you move past that mindset and focus on your own journey, growing from your unique strengths.
- Build from strength, alignment, and truth: Starting a practice isn't just about business. It's about creating a space where your values align with your work. This book will help you clarify what matters most and integrate those values into your practice.

To do any of this effectively, your foundation must be solid. Like any stable structure, your practice needs a solid foundation. Think of it this way: if you were building a house, the first thing you'd need is a strong foundation. Without it, the entire structure could crumble. The same is true for your practice. If it isn't rooted in clarity and purpose, it may falter when challenges arise.

That foundation begins with understanding why you're building your practice in the first place.

Before moving into practical steps, pause here—this is a reflective moment meant to clarify your internal compass.

Here are the key elements to strengthen it:

- **Your Vision:** What's your ultimate goal for your practice? What does success look like to you, and how does it align with your values?
- **Your Mission:** Why do you care about the work you do? What brings meaning and fulfillment to your practice?
- **Your Purpose:** What's the deeper reason you want to step into leadership? This is your core anchor—the why that keeps you going when things get tough.

Once this foundation is in place, the logistical steps that come next begin to feel meaningful rather than overwhelming. The legal paperwork, systems, and marketing won't feel like disconnected tasks; they'll feel purposeful, all aligned with your bigger mission.

The Thriving Practice Success Pyramid

Think of building your private practice like constructing a pyramid. At the base is Purpose—the foundation of everything. On top of that is Structure—the systems and processes that keep your practice running smoothly. At the very top is Visibility—how you ensure people know about your practice. Each of these three layers builds on the one before it, creating a stable foundation for growth.

Let's break down each layer and explore how they work together to help you build a thriving practice.

Purpose: The Foundation

Your practice needs a strong foundation, and that foundation starts with purpose. This is the why behind everything you do—the reason you wanted to start your practice in the first place. Without a clear purpose, it's easy to lose direction or feel like you're simply going through the motions. Your purpose keeps you grounded when challenges arise.

Your purpose should include:

- **Your passion for medicine or mental health:** What inspired you to choose this career? Is it your desire to help others, your love of problem-solving, or your passion for healing? Remembering why you entered this field will help you stay connected to your why when things get tough.
- **Your vision for patient care:** How do you want to treat your patients? What kind of care do you want to offer that's different from what's already out there? Your vision shapes how you build relationships and deliver the best possible care.
- **Your personal values:** What do you stand for—honesty, integrity, compassion? Your values should guide how you run your practice and interact with others. When your practice aligns with your core values, it naturally attracts the right patients and partners.

Purpose is the foundation because it anchors you. It helps you stay steady even when circumstances feel chaotic. When you have a clear purpose, everything you do gains direction.

Structure: The Middle Layer

Once you've defined your purpose, the next step is to build your structure—the operational backbone of your practice. This includes the systems, processes, and tools that keep everything running efficiently. Without a strong structure, even the best intentions can unravel.

Structure should include:

- **Legal and financial setup:** Begin by establishing your business entity (such as an LLC or PLLC) and getting your finances in order. Open a dedicated business bank account, secure proper insurance, and create a solid plan for taxes.
- **Operational systems:** How will you manage patient appointments, billing, and records? Scheduling software, billing systems, and Electronic Medical Records (EMR) tools are essential for ensuring smooth operations and allowing you to focus on patient care.
- **Workflows and protocols:** Standardized procedures are key to delivering consistent care. For example, define how you'll handle patient intake, treatment planning, and follow-ups. Clear workflows help maintain quality, reduce confusion, and support team efficiency.

Structure is the framework that holds your practice together, freeing you to focus on what matters most—caring for your patients. Without it, your operations can feel chaotic, making growth difficult.

Once internal systems are stable, attention can move outward.

Visibility: The Pinnacle

At the top of your pyramid is Visibility—ensuring people know who you are and what you offer. It's how you attract patients, build credibility, and earn trust in your community.

This final layer focuses on connection and outreach.

Visibility includes:

- **Marketing and branding:** What do you want people to think of when they hear your practice's name? Develop a brand identity that communicates your values and expertise. Your marketing strategy might include your website, social media, and outreach efforts.
- **Community engagement:** Build relationships within your local community and professional network. Attend events, partner with other healthcare providers, and get involved in local initiatives. These connections establish trust and make it easier for people to find you.
- **Online presence:** In today's digital world, online visibility is crucial. Patients often search for providers online first, so having a professional website and an active social media presence is essential. Online reviews also build credibility and help new patients trust your practice.

Visibility connects you with the patients who need your services most. You may have a strong sense of purpose and a solid structure, but without visibility, your practice won't grow. This layer ensures people can find and trust you as the right provider for them.

Bringing It All Together: A Unified Approach

Having explored each layer individually, the final step is integration. These three layers—Purpose, Structure, and Visibility—work together to create a strong, sustainable practice. Think of them as a cycle:

- **Purpose** guides everything you do, keeping you aligned and focused on what matters most.
- **Structure** allows your practice to run efficiently, delivering great care while supporting growth.
- **Visibility** connects you with the world outside your office, helping your practice reach those who need your expertise.

When these layers are in place and functioning together, you'll have a stable foundation to build upon—one that supports excellent patient care, operational smoothness, and values-driven growth.

Key Takeaways

- Purpose is the foundation. It gives you clarity and direction, helping you make aligned decisions.
- Structure ensures your practice runs smoothly, covering everything from legal setup to workflows.
- Visibility connects your practice to the world through marketing, community engagement, and online presence.
- When Purpose, Structure, and Visibility align, you'll be well on your way to building a successful and sustainable practice.

Exercise: Know Your Why

This exercise is intentionally reflective and designed to clarify your internal foundation before action begins.

Before diving into the tactical steps of building your practice, pause and reflect on your "why." Your "why" is the bedrock of your journey. It will anchor you and keep you moving forward, especially when things get tough.

Here are three questions to guide your reflection. Answer them thoughtfully, and keep them visible as reminders of your purpose:

1. **Why are you choosing private practice now?** What's motivating you to take this step? Is it the desire for greater autonomy, to serve your patients more directly, or to reclaim your time and live life on your own terms? Whatever the reason, get clear on why now is the right time for you to start this journey.
2. **What do you want your practice to feel like day to day?** Imagine your ideal practice. What does a typical day look like? Is it calm, fulfilling, and balanced, or energetic and fast-paced? Your vision should align with your lifestyle goals. Be intentional about what you want, and let that vision shape your decisions as you build.
3. **Who are you most excited to help, and why?** This question defines your target audience. Is there a specific group you feel called to serve—children, underserved communities, or those recovering

from addiction or trauma? Your ideal patient demographic should resonate with your mission and values. A clear focus helps you build a practice that is not only successful but deeply fulfilling.

Write down your answers and keep them nearby. Refer to them often, especially during challenging times. They will help guide your decisions and keep you aligned with your purpose.

As clarity increases, it's natural for resistance to surface.

Once you've connected with your "why," it's common for doubts and fears to surface, which is part of the process.

Common Fears, and How to Face Them

It's natural to experience fear when starting something new. Launching a private practice means stepping into the unknown, and with that often comes uncertainty. You might find yourself wondering:

- What if I fail?
- What if I don't have enough clients?
- What if I'm not good enough to run a business?

These fears are normal, and you're not alone in feeling them. Every successful entrepreneur has faced doubt—the difference is their willingness to feel the fear and move forward anyway.

Here's how to face your fears:

- Fear of Failure: Failure isn't the end; it's part of the process. Every great entrepreneur has failed along the way. Failure is feedback, not a reflection of your worth. Use it to learn, adapt, and grow stronger.
- **Fear of Not Having Enough Clients:** Clients are out there; they're simply waiting for the right provider who understands their needs and values. Building visibility and trust takes time, but when you focus on delivering value and consistency, your client base will grow. Start small, stay steady, and trust the process.
- **Fear of Not Being Good Enough:** You are already qualified. Your education, experience, and heart for helping others have prepared you for this. Confidence builds through action—even small steps forward will strengthen your belief in yourself.

These fears don't have to control you. When you face them with courage and resilience, you'll discover that the confidence you need has been within you all along, waiting to be activated.

Final Words Before We Begin

You are the founder now—the CEO, the author of your success. You're allowed to succeed. You're allowed to build wealth. You're allowed to feel peace.

Let this chapter mark your turning point. You don't need more time; you need belief. You are exactly who your future clients are waiting for.

Next: Let's lay the foundation. Your practice begins now.

Chapter 2: From Worker to Owner—Your Mindset Shift

"Success is not about what you do for a living, but what you create with your life. You have the power to redefine your path, break free from limitations, and build something that's entirely your own." – Oprah Winfrey

Medical training is built on hierarchy. From day one, you're taught to defer to your attendings, your program, and the system. You're told when to show up, how long to stay, and who decides your future. Your entire career, up to this point, has revolved around following orders, absorbing knowledge, and waiting for approval.

But once you graduate, something shifts. You're no longer just a trainee. You're a doctor. You've earned the title, the knowledge, and the respect that come with it. You're a leader in your field, capable of making life-altering decisions for your patients. And if you choose, you're also a business owner—someone who can build something of their own.

This chapter is about breaking free from the ingrained narrative that says, "I'm not ready," "I'm not good with business," or "I need permission to lead." These aren't truths; they are learned beliefs shaped by years in hierarchical training environments. And the unfortunate reality is that they keep brilliant doctors confined to systems that limit their potential, their impact, and their autonomy. It's time to rewrite that script.

Rewriting the Script: From Worker to Owner

Old Script: "I'm not qualified to run a practice."

New Script: "I'm already qualified to care for people, and I can learn the rest."

As a medical professional, you have spent years honing your craft. You've become an expert in diagnosing, treating, and managing patient care. The truth is, you are already qualified. You have the skills and the compassion to help people—this is what matters most in healthcare.

The business side of running a practice is simply another skill to learn, much like mastering a new procedure or treatment plan. Business is learnable. You don't need to wait until you have all the answers. By taking one step at a time, seeking guidance when needed, and building your knowledge gradually, you can run a thriving practice. It may seem daunting at first, but with the same focus and determination you brought to your medical training, you'll adapt quickly.

You've already proven that you can learn complex skills. The mindset that carried you through residency will serve you here too.

Old Script: "I didn't go to business school."

New Script: "Business is learnable. My mission is priceless."

One of the biggest myths in entrepreneurship is that success requires a business degree. While formal business education can be helpful, it is not required to build a thriving practice.

Consider that many of the most successful entrepreneurs learned by doing—experimenting, adapting, and refining along the way. They took calculated risks, learned from setbacks, and improved through experience. You don't need an MBA to own a practice. You need clarity, dedication, and a mission.

Your mission—to serve your patients and create a space for meaningful healing—is priceless. When your purpose leads, business strategy follows.

Old Script: "What if I fail?"

New Script: "What if I succeed?"

This is often where the mindset shift truly begins. Fear of failure is natural, especially when the work is personal. But failure is not final; it is part of growth. Every entrepreneur encounters it. What matters is how you rise.

Rather than fearing possible setbacks, see them as steps in your evolution. The worst-case scenario is rarely as catastrophic as the mind imagines. And the best-case scenario? You build something deeply aligned with your values, your expertise, and your vision for care.

You won't know unless you take the step.

You don't have to become someone else to own your practice. You don't need to mimic extroverted entrepreneurs or corporate executives. What you need is to step more fully into who you already are.

The same qualities that make you a great physician—your commitment, your resilience, your empathy, your discipline—are the qualities that make strong practice owners. You've already developed the mindset required for leadership; now it's about expanding its scope.

Starting your own practice isn't about changing yourself. It's about growing into the fuller expression of your calling—as a healer, a leader, and a professional shaping your own path.

The Mindset of a Practice Owner

Transitioning from a doctor to a practice owner requires a shift in mindset. As a clinician, you were taught to follow orders, defer to the system, and work within established boundaries. But as a practice owner, you get to make the rules. You have the opportunity to design your own practice, create a culture that reflects your values, and build a business that supports your life and goals.

Before we get into the practical steps, it helps to shift how you see yourself—not just as a provider, but as a leader and builder.

Here's how to step into the mindset of a successful practice owner:

- Be the CEO of Your Practice: Shift from thinking like an employee to thinking like an owner. You are the leader now. Make decisions with confidence and take responsibility for both the successes and the challenges.
- Embrace Your Role as a Problem Solver: As a doctor, you already solve complex problems daily. Now, you'll apply that same analytical thinking to the business side—managing finances, attracting patients, refining systems, and improving workflows. You have the ability to find solutions.
- Stay Committed to Learning: You may not have business school training, but business skills are learnable. Through reading, mentorship, courses, or hands-on experience, each step you take adds to your understanding. Stay curious and adaptable.
- Stay True to Your Mission: Your purpose—to provide excellent care—is the core of your practice. When decisions feel overwhelming, return to your mission. It will keep you clear, focused, and grounded.

The shift from being a doctor in a hierarchical system to becoming a practice owner requires more than a new title. It's a full mindset transformation. Moving from employee to entrepreneur means changing how you think about your work, your value, and your measure of success.

Old Identity → Limiting Beliefs → Transitional Scripts → Ownership Identity

- Old Identity: As a doctor, you've been conditioned to follow orders, defer to authority, and work within a defined system. You've been trained to operate as part of a structure, not necessarily to lead one.
- Limiting Beliefs: You may notice thoughts such as: "I'm not ready to lead." "I'm not good with business." "I need permission to take the next step." These beliefs keep you anchored to the past. They are learned patterns, not truths.
- Transitional Scripts: This is where you begin replacing limiting beliefs with more accurate, empowered statements:
- **Old Script:** "I'm not good with business."
- **New Script:** "Business is learnable, and I can learn it."
- **Old Script:** "I need permission to lead."
- **New Script:** "I am a leader, and I don't need permission."
- Ownership Identity: The final shift is claiming your identity as an owner. You are no longer simply a clinician following direction. You are the CEO of your career, responsible for your decisions, growth, and trajectory.

Shifting into entrepreneurial identity shows up in your daily choices:

- Saying no to work that drains you: Prioritize work aligned with your values.
- Setting your own schedule: You decide how your time is used.
- Naming your fees without apologizing: Your expertise is valuable—own that.
- Taking time off when needed: You design a practice that supports your life.

Ownership isn't a title. It's a decision. Becoming a practice owner is an ongoing choice. It's about stewardship—protecting your vision and guiding it forward. No one else will advocate for it the way you will.

The Transition from Employee to Entrepreneur

This transition involves rethinking how you define productivity, success, and autonomy. For years, you may have been conditioned to seek approval and operate within prescribed limits. Now, you decide the structure. You build the culture. You design a practice that reflects your mission.

The ownership mindset isn't just about running a business; it's about leading with purpose. When you claim ownership, you give yourself permission to create a practice that reflects your values and supports your vision for care.

Once you step into your leadership role, your possibilities expand. You are prepared for this next chapter, and you have everything you need to move forward.

The first mindset shift you need to make is recognizing that you already possess the most important qualifications to own your practice: clinical competence and the ability to help people. These are the core skills that matter most. You've spent years training to be a doctor, and that experience is priceless. It's what sets you apart and allows you to make a real difference in the lives of your patients.

You don't need perfection. You need value. Many clinicians struggle with impostor syndrome—that feeling that you're not truly qualified or deserving of success. This is especially common among high achievers accustomed to constant evaluation during medical training. That environment can create the belief that you must be flawless before taking your next step.

But entrepreneurship operates differently.

- Perfection isn't the goal: What matters is the value you deliver. You don't need every answer; you just need to help your patients solve real problems.
- You don't need to know everything: Business is a skill that develops through practice. Starting is what allows you to learn.

- You don't need permission: There is no "perfect moment." The only approval that matters is your own.

  Once you release the pressure to be perfect, you open the door to growth, movement, and possibility.

  Entrepreneurship is about having the courage to begin with what you already know, and learning along the way.

- Start small: You don't need a complete business plan. Begin with one patient, one offering, one decision.
- Learn as you grow: Every new challenge will teach you something important. Progress comes through action.
- Embrace imperfection: Confidence is built through doing, not waiting.

Building Confidence in Yourself as an Entrepreneur

In medicine, you were trained to care for others. As an entrepreneur, you must extend that same trust and belief to yourself. You already have what you need to begin; now, you're learning how to apply it in a new context.

- You are capable: Your clinical skills are a strong and sufficient foundation.
- You are valuable: Your knowledge and compassion are what people seek in a healthcare provider.
- You can learn as you go: Growth happens through action, not preparation alone.

The first step to owning your practice is recognizing that you don't need to be perfect, you don't need permission, and you don't need to have everything figured out from the start. What you need is the willingness to begin and the openness to learn along the way.

The value you provide matters far more than perfection. Start with what you know, take the first step, and allow the rest to unfold. You are ready to move forward.

In medical training, you're often taught to operate from a scarcity mindset, believing opportunities are limited, competition is constant, and external validation determines your worth. In contrast, the abundance mindset of successful entrepreneurs teaches that:

- Value creation is unlimited: There is always room for innovation and improvement.
- Collaboration can outperform competition: Working with others often leads to better outcomes than trying to outdo them.
- True security comes from your ability to serve effectively: When you provide real value, success follows.

From Employee Thinking to Ownership Thinking

Moving from clinician to practice owner requires a fundamental mindset shift—from task execution to system leadership, from security to value creation.

In clinical roles, your focus is on individual patient care. As an owner, your perspective expands:

- How does each decision affect the overall business?
- How do your systems shape the patient experience?
- How do your marketing strategies guide the right patients to you?

This shift doesn't pull you away from care—it enables you to provide care more effectively.

Employees focus on completing tasks efficiently. Owners build systems that function even when they are not directly involved. This allows you to scale your impact and reclaim time in your schedule. With this transition comes a new relationship to risk. As an employee, avoiding mistakes is emphasized. As an owner, growth requires you to:

- Make decisions with incomplete information.
- Experiment and learn from results.
- Take strategic—not reckless—risks.

Ownership also reshapes how you think internally:

- Employee mindset: "What do they want me to do?"
- Ownership mindset: "What needs to be done, and how can I improve it?"
- Employee mindset: Looks for security through compliance.
- Ownership mindset: Builds security through value creation.
- Employee mindset: Waits for opportunities.
- Ownership mindset: Creates opportunities through action.

Success begins internally. You do not need:

- Approval from former colleagues.
- Immediate support from family.
- Permission to pursue your vision.

What you do need is:

- Clarity about your goals.
- Commitment to your values.
- Courage to act despite uncertainty.

This mindset shift is gradual and develops through experience, not theory.

Building a Sustainable Practice Through an Abundance Mindset

Ownership also requires a shift from scarcity to sustainability.

A scarcity mindset may show up as:

- Undercharging for your services.
- Overworking to prove your worth.
- Hesitating to set boundaries with patients or staff.

An abundance mindset supports:

- Pricing your services appropriately.
- Working sustainably to prevent burnout.
- Setting clear boundaries to protect yourself and your patients.

You cannot support others if you burn out, struggle financially, or are forced to close your doors. Taking care of your business is part of taking care of your patients. A sustainable model ensures consistent, high-quality care without sacrificing your well-being.

Give yourself space to grow. Be patient. Celebrate small progress. Learn from setbacks—they are part of the journey. Surround yourself with others who understand the entrepreneurial path. Every successful practice owner has navigated these same adjustments.

Your clinical training has already prepared you. It gave you:

- Strong problem-solving skills.
- Emotional intelligence.
- The ability to perform under pressure.
- Empathy and communication.
- How to build trust.

Your commitment to helping others fuels your purpose—and that purpose will carry you through challenges.

The question is not whether you're qualified to own a practice.

The real question is: Are you willing to step into your power and build the professional life you want?

If you're reading this, you already know the answer.

Building Your Legacy

You're not just starting a practice; you're building a legacy.

History offers powerful reminders that mindset, purpose, and persistence shape lasting impact more than circumstances ever could. Consider the journey of Ben Carson, who was raised by a single mother with only a third-grade education and struggled academically in his early years. Over time, he developed a deep belief in education and disciplined work—an internal shift that guided him to become one of the most respected neurosurgeons in the world. Known for pioneering complex procedures such as the successful separation of conjoined twins, his story illustrates how a change in perspective can transform challenges into stepping stones for remarkable achievement.

A similar commitment to purpose shaped the path of Patch Adams. His compassionate and unconventional approach to medicine—emphasizing laughter, emotional support, and human connection alongside clinical care—was initially met with resistance from traditional institutions. Yet by trusting his vision, he founded the Gesundheit! Institute and helped redefine how emotional wellness is valued in healthcare. His journey shows that when one fully commits to meaningful work, even unconventional paths can flourish.

Persistence in the face of rejection also defined the rise of Laura Schlessinger. Despite numerous early setbacks, she remained committed to sharing her message of practical, direct relationship guidance. Through radio, books, and podcasts, she grew into a trusted voice for millions—demonstrating how authenticity and consistency can transform obstacles into influence.

Equally compelling is the example of Betty Williams, whose life reflected perseverance in service of others. Raised in a low-income community and navigating the challenges of single motherhood, she remained determined to support vulnerable populations. Her work as a nurse and advocate for patients affected by HIV/AIDS earned national recognition and stands as a testament to how compassion and commitment can drive meaningful change.

These stories remind us that legacy is not built by circumstance alone, but by the willingness to pursue purpose with courage, resilience, and conviction.

Your Inner Dialogue

Your inner dialogue is powerful. It's the voice that shapes your confidence, your decisions, and your direction. For many of us, that voice is influenced by old stories and limiting beliefs—narratives that keep us playing small. Today, we're going to rewrite those beliefs and shift toward ownership, confidence, and possibility.

Small exercise

To begin this shift, we'll use a simple exercise designed to help you reclaim your internal narrative. Write down the top three beliefs that are holding you back from owning your career. Then rewrite each one with strength and conviction. Speak them out loud. This is about taking conscious control of your story—not waiting for change, but creating it.

Limiting Belief #1: "I'm not ready."

New Belief: "I've never been more ready to reclaim my path."

- You've spent years building your expertise and overcoming challenges. Your experiences, training, and resilience have prepared you for this moment. Every step has led you here; now is the time to step forward.

Limiting Belief #2: "I don't have the business skills."

New Belief: "Business is learnable, and I am committed to mastering it."

- You may not have a business degree, but capability isn't defined by titles. Business is a skill—just like any clinical or procedural skill you've already mastered. You've learned complex systems before. You can learn this too.

Limiting Belief #3: "What if I fail?"

New Belief: "What if I succeed beyond my expectations?"

- Fear of failure often keeps us from starting, but failure is simply information—a step toward refinement. Consider the possibility of success: creating the practice you envision, offering the care you believe in, and seeing lives transform. Let possibility lead rather than fear.

Limiting Belief #4: "I need permission to start."

New Belief: "I give myself permission to create the future I want."

- Your goals do not require external validation. You are fully capable of deciding when to begin. Your future expands the moment you choose to act.

Limiting Belief #5: "I'm afraid of what others will think."

New Belief: "I will surround myself with people who support my vision, and the rest will fall into place."

- The fear of judgment is human, but your purpose is bigger than other people's opinions. Those aligned with your values will recognize your drive and respect your commitment. Stay focused on your mission—your belief in your path matters more than anyone's doubt.

Final Words

This is the chapter where you stop waiting and start claiming. It's time to stop shrinking. It's time to stop delaying. Ownership starts now. The beliefs that have kept you stuck are no longer relevant. The voice of doubt can no longer hold you back. You are the CEO of your career, and that starts with taking ownership of your thoughts. Speak these new beliefs out loud with power, conviction, and confidence. You're no longer waiting for permission. You are taking action today. Let's Go. This is the moment you've been waiting for. Step into your power and create the practice you've always dreamed of. You've got this — let's make it happen.

Chapter 3: Legal & Operational Launch Essentials

"I'm convinced that about half of what separates successful entrepreneurs from the non-successful ones is pure perseverance." – Steve Jobs

Starting your private practice legally doesn't require a law degree—it requires clear steps and persistence. This chapter breaks down the essentials into an actionable checklist, from entity formation to EMR selection. We'll cover nationwide requirements with state-specific notes, ensuring you're compliant and ready to launch.

Remember, laws evolve, so consult a local attorney or accountant for personalized advice. Let's build your foundation.

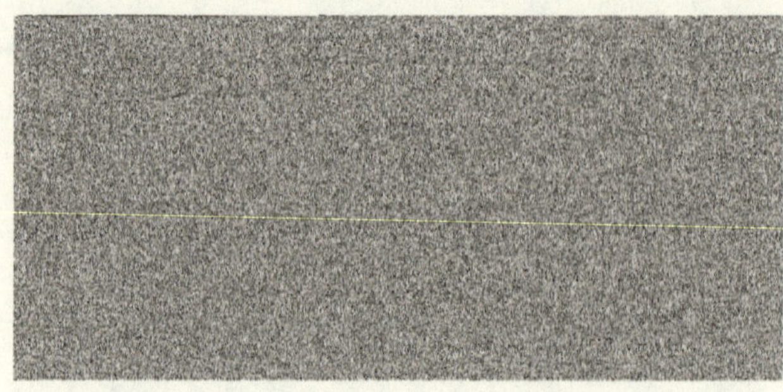

Step 1: Choose Your Business Entity (PLLC or PC)

Select a Professional Limited Liability Company (PLLC) or Professional Corporation (PC) to protect your personal assets while complying with professional licensing rules. Most states allow PLLCs for mental health providers; some require PCs. (Refer to Appendix A for State Entity Formation Guide)

Example Scenario: Texas vs. California vs. New York Entity Formation

Example:

Sarah (Texas), Daniel (California), and Priya (New York) all start private practices the same month.

Sarah – Texas (PLLC friendly, fast processing)

Sarah files a PLLC online with the Texas Secretary of State for ~$300. She does not need prior board approval. Within 5 business days, she receives confirmation, applies for her EIN the same day, and opens her bank account that week. Total time: **10 days**. Total cost: **~$450**.

Daniel – California (Professional Corporation required)

California does not allow PLLCs for many licensed professionals. Daniel must form a **Professional Corporation (PC)**. He first submits paperwork to the licensing board for approval before filing Articles of Incorporation. He pays ~$1000 in total fees (state filing, legal templates, publication requirement in some counties). Processing time: **6–8 weeks**.

Priya – New York (Education Department involvement)

Priya cannot file directly with the Secretary of State. She must first submit forms to the **NY State Education Department**, wait for approval, complete a notarized affidavit, and then file formation paperwork. Total time: **8–12 weeks**. Total cost: **~$700**.

Lesson: The entity step that takes one provider 10 days may take another 3 months. This is normal, not a mistake.

Step 2: Open a Business Bank Account

Separate your personal and business finances to simplify taxes and protect assets. Use your EIN, entity documents, and professional license to open an account at a bank like Chase or Wells Fargo. Look for low-fee options with online banking.

Cost Breakdown: What You Actually Need to Open Your Account

You will be asked for:

- EIN confirmation letter (free)
- Articles of Organization/Incorporation
- Professional license
- Operating Agreement (many banks require this even if your state doesn't)

Typical startup banking costs:

- Minimum deposit: $100–$500
- Monthly fee: $0–$25 (waived with balance)
- Business debit card: free

Pro Tip: Many new owners forget to bring their Operating Agreement and must reschedule the appointment.

Step 3: Secure Malpractice Insurance

Protect yourself from lawsuits with professional liability insurance. Providers like HPSO, Berxi, or CM&F offer tailored policies for mental health professionals. Coverage typically starts at $1 million per incident/$3 million aggregate. Compare quotes and ensure it covers telehealth if applicable.

Troubleshooting: Why Quotes Vary from $120/year to $800/year

If you receive widely different quotes, it's usually due to:

- Indicating you prescribe controlled substances
- Selecting telehealth across state lines
- Choosing claims-made vs. occurrence coverage
- Selecting higher limits than needed

Example:

A therapist in Florida quoted $140/year. A psychiatric NP in Illinois quoted $780/year because of prescribing and telehealth coverage.

Always verify the policy includes telehealth and license defense coverage.

Step 4: Register for Taxes and Handle Receipts

Register for state and federal taxes using your EIN. Use software like QuickBooks for tracking. For receipts (e.g., business expenses like office supplies or marketing), scan and organize them digitally via apps like Expensify or Shoeboxed. Deduct eligible expenses (e.g., EMR subscriptions, continuing education) to reduce tax liability—consult an accountant for compliance. Keep receipts for 7 years per IRS guidelines.

Example Monthly Expense Snapshot (Solo Practice)

Typical monthly expenses:

- EMR: $39–$99
- Malpractice insurance: $15–$60
- Virtual office: $50–$120
- Google Workspace/HIPAA email: $12
- Scheduling/automation tools: $15
- Office rental (1 day/week): $200–$400

Total baseline overhead: $350–$700/month

This is far lower than most expect and shows how lean a private practice can start.

Step 5: Obtain Necessary Licenses and Certifications

Renew your state medical/therapy license and ensure any specialty certifications (e.g., board certification in psychiatry) are current. If offering telehealth across states, join the Interstate Medical Licensure Compact or Psychology Interjurisdictional Compact.

Step 6: Set Up HIPAA Compliance

Protect patient privacy with HIPAA-compliant tools. Sign Business Associate Agreements (BAAs) with vendors (e.g., EMR providers). Use secure email like Hushmail and train yourself on data security.

Common Mistake Scenario

Example:

A provider uses regular Gmail to send intake forms. A patient later requests records, and the provider realizes no BAA exists with Google for that account. This becomes a HIPAA risk.

Fix: Upgrade to **Google Workspace**, sign the BAA, and use encrypted email moving forward.

Step 7: Apply for a DEA Number (If Prescribing)

If prescribing controlled substances, obtain a DEA number.

- Visit dea.gov to apply online.
- Provide state license, business address, and credentials.
- Fee: ~$888 for 3 years.

Process: 4-6 weeks. Renew every 3 years.

- State variations: Check Prescription Monitoring Programs (PMPs) and additional rules.

Troubleshooting DEA Delays

DEA applications are often delayed because:

- Business address doesn't match license address
- State license renewal is pending
- Incorrect business activity selected

Many delays add **4–6 extra weeks**. Double-check every field before submitting.

Step 8: Obtain Your National Provider Identifier (NPI)

Your NPI is a 10-digit ID for billing and claims. Apply free at nppes.cms.hhs.gov. Include it on all forms.

Step 9: Starter EMRs for Launching Your Practice

Your EMR is your digital backbone. When you're just getting started, prioritize ease of use, affordability, and simplicity. Look for systems that reduce overwhelm and let you focus on building momentum. For example:

- SimplePractice: User-friendly for therapists.
- TheraNest: Customizable.

- TherapyNotes: For detailed charting.
- OpenEMR: Budget-friendly open-source.

Ensure HIPAA compliance and test with free trials.

Scenario: Choosing the Wrong EMR Costs Time

Example:

A therapist chooses an EMR based on price alone. After 3 months, they realize it lacks automated reminders, integrated billing, and telehealth. They switch systems and must manually transfer 40 patient charts.

Lesson: Use the free trials. Test scheduling, reminders, notes, and billing before committing.

Step 10: Choose a Prescribing Platform

Streamline prescriptions with:

- DrFirst: Real-time history and interactions.
- Practice Fusion: Affordable for small practices.
- MDTech: Integrates with EHRs.
- RXNT: Comprehensive for medium practices.

Step 11: Office Space Considerations

Minimize overhead: Rent one day/week via Regus. Use virtual offices for addresses. Avoid sharing personal numbers—use Google Voice. Respond promptly to build trust.

Cost Comparison: Full Office vs. Shared Space

Full-time lease: $1,200/month + utilities + furniture

1 day/week Regus rental: ~$300/month, fully furnished

In year one, this saves **~$10,000** while patient volume builds.

Key Tips:

- Rent office one day per week to reduce overhead. Regus and co-working spaces are great for this.
- Avoid using your home address. Use a virtual office instead.
- Don't give out your personal phone number. Use Google Voice or a secure platform.
- Be responsive and professional; early trust builds long-term loyalty.
- Make small, thoughtful touches like bottled water or clean design part of the experience.

Consider focusing on a specific area such as trauma, ADHD, OCD, or eating disorders. Join niche-specific associations to deepen your credibility. Specialization not only builds faster referrals but also leads to better outcomes and personal satisfaction.

If you're in New York:

- File with the NY State Education Department.
- Complete a notarized affidavit.
- Submit through the Department of Professions.
- Visit op.nysed.gov for detailed instructions.

Systems That Scale with Sanity

One of the biggest mistakes new practice owners make is trying to manage everything manually. Hours get lost answering emails, scheduling appointments by hand, and chasing down payments. That path leads straight to burnout.

Systems are your solution. They handle the behind-the-scenes tasks so you can focus on delivering exceptional care. A thriving practice runs smoothly not because of hustle, but because of smart systems.

What Systems Can Do for You

- Save Time: Automate repetitive tasks so you can focus on patient care.
- Reduce Stress: Streamline workflows to create calmer, more organized days.
- Improve Patient Experience: Offer seamless scheduling, communication, and follow-up.
- Grow Without Burnout: Scale your practice sustainably and with balance.

If your practice depends entirely on your daily energy and availability, it isn't scalable. Let's fix that.

Lead Generation → Intake → Appointment → Billing → Follow-Up → Retention

System Failure Scenario (What Happens Without Automation)

A new practice owner manually schedules via text, sends invoices separately, and tracks appointments in a notebook. Within 2 months:

- Missed appointments increase
- Payments are delayed
- Intake forms are incomplete
- Stress rises

After switching to EMR automation, no-shows drop by 60% and payments become automatic.

EMR (Electronic Medical Record) Systems

As your practice grows, you'll quickly see that well-designed systems don't just save time; they protect your peace. Choosing a reliable EMR is one of the most important investments you'll make. Look for something HIPAA-compliant, user-friendly, and suited to your specialty.

EMRs for Scaling

As your practice expands, your systems need to support scale — additional providers, integrated billing, telehealth, prescribing, and operational efficiency.

- SimplePractice: Intuitive, all-in-one system with scheduling, notes, billing, and telehealth.
- Luminello: Designed for psychiatry with built-in e-prescribing.
- Jane App: Ideal for group practices and wellness providers.
- TheraNest: Great for small or solo practices.
- Kareo: Excellent for independent practices seeking scalability.

Scheduling Tools

Once your EMR is in place, efficient scheduling keeps your days predictable and calm. Efficient scheduling = less chaos.

Options:

- Built-In EMR Calendars: Integrated with patient records.
- Calendly: Patient self-booking with auto-reminders.
- Acuity Scheduling: Custom forms, payments, reminders.
- Zocdoc: Good visibility but may cost more if volume is low.

Pro Tip: I personally use SimplePractice; it handles scheduling, reminders, billing, and notes effortlessly.

Set Your Boundaries and Charge What You're Worth

As your systems take shape, it becomes even more important to protect your energy. You are not on call 24/7. You deserve rest, space, and fair compensation.

Your pricing reflects your years of training and the value you provide. Set non-negotiables: lunch, admin time, and breaks are essential. Automation helps, but boundaries sustain your well-being. You're not just a provider; you're a CEO. Own your worth.

Create a Healthy Practice Culture

Strong systems allow you to build a culture that feels grounded and sustainable. Boundaries aren't walls; they are frameworks for sustainability. Lead with respect—for your time, your values, your vision. When you uphold your boundaries, others follow. Build a culture rooted in clarity, trust, and mutual respect.

A smooth first session begins with strong preparation behind the scenes.

Before First Session:

- Collect: Informed consent, privacy policies, and intake paperwork.
- Automate: Use EMR or tools like JotForm or Typeform. Time is your most valuable asset. Protect it.

Link Stripe, Square, or Zelle to your EMR. Offer autopay or saved cards. Set clear cancellation and no-show policies up front. Use EMR's text or email reminders. Reduce no-shows with confirmable texts: "Reply Y to confirm."

Bonus Tip: Include your reschedule policy in each reminder.

As your system grows, security must grow with it.

Data Protection Checklist

- Enable 2FA (Two-Factor Authentication).
- Backup using encrypted cloud tools (Google Workspace, Dropbox).
- Use HIPAA-compliant email (e.g., Hushmail).
- Sign BAAs with vendors who handle PHI.

A secure practice is a trusted practice. You don't need to know how to code, but you must lead with strategy. As your systems strengthen, clarity becomes essential.

What to Automate:

- Intake forms.
- Appointment reminders.
- Billing.
- Follow-up emails.

What to Delegate:

- Scheduling.
- Admin support.
- Insurance (if applicable).

What to Eliminate:

- Energy-draining tasks that don't serve patients or growth.

Be the visionary. Systems do the work; you lead the mission.

Startup Timeline Reality Check

Realistic timeline from idea to first patient:

- Entity formation: 2–12 weeks (state dependent)
- EIN/Bank/Insurance: 1 week
- EMR/HIPAA setup: 1 week
- Licensing/DEA/NPI: 2–8 weeks

Most providers see their first patient **60–120 days** after starting the process. This is normal and expected.

Steps to Finding Affordable Lawyers:

- **Inquire About Sliding Scale Fees:** Many attorneys offer fees based on income—don't hesitate to ask.
- **Negotiate Payment Plans:** Some lawyers will work on payment plans or hourly rates depending on your financial situation.
- **Look for Pro Bono or Volunteer Legal Services:** Some lawyers offer pro bono services through organizations such as the American Bar Association or state bar associations.
- **Leverage Local Universities and Law Schools:** Many law schools have clinics where law students provide services under supervision, often free or low-cost.

Final Words

Starting your private practice legally becomes manageable when you break it down into clear, intentional steps. By following this checklist and understanding each piece of the puzzle, you've created a solid, compliant foundation. Because every state has its own requirements, continuing to research and confirm state-specific regulations ensures you remain aligned and protected.

This process can feel overwhelming at times. I know that firsthand. I've walked through it multiple times, which is why it's laid out here step by step, with diagrams to support visual learners. Take it one task at a time. Take breaks when you need to. It's not a race. Some states take four to six months to process filings, and patience is simply part of the journey.

The hardest part is now behind you. The paperwork is complete, the legal steps are in place, and the structure for success is set. From here forward, resist the urge to micromanage. Trust the systems you've built. Let technology handle the administrative weight so you can focus on relationships, care, and impact. Technology isn't replacing you; it's freeing you.

Strong systems simplify your life. Healthy boundaries protect your energy. Leadership gives your practice purpose. You're not just building a business; you're building a sustainable life and a meaningful legacy.

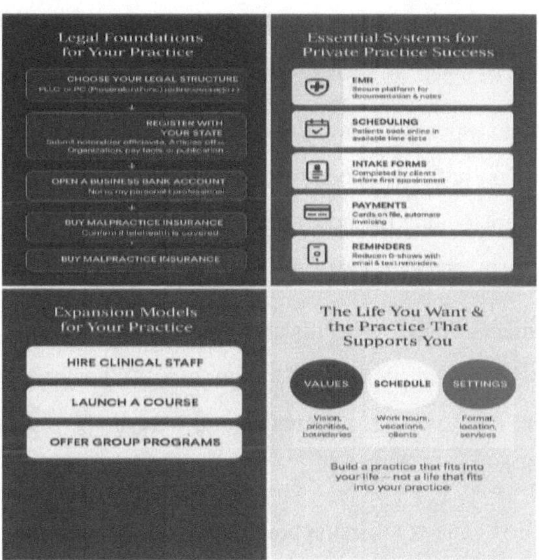

You've laid the groundwork. Now it's time to bring your vision to life, lead with confidence, and build the practice patients trust. Ready for the next step? Let's move on to Chapter 4.

Chapter 4: Branding That Connects and Converts

"People do not buy goods and services. They buy relations, stories, and magic." —Seth Godin

Branding is often seen as just a logo, a color scheme, or a tagline, but in reality, it's so much more. Branding is about trust. It's the feeling someone gets when they land on your website, read your bio, or hear your name. It's about how you make people feel, not just what they see. Your brand is the emotional handshake between you and your ideal client—the first impression that tells them, "You're in the right place."

This perspective comes from observing how patients respond emotionally, long before any clinical interaction begins.

In healthcare, branding is crucial. Patients are not just searching for clinical expertise; they are searching for someone they can trust, someone who understands their needs, and someone who will listen. They want to feel connected to their provider, especially as they often come to you during vulnerable moments in their lives. Your brand should reflect that human connection, showing empathy and care in addition to your qualifications.

When you create a brand that speaks to your ideal clients, you're not just selling a service; you're offering peace of mind. You're offering comfort in a time of uncertainty and guidance through life's challenges. Patients are looking for more than a skilled provider; they're looking for someone who will see them, hear them, and care for them.

That's why branding matters so much in healthcare. Your brand tells your patients: "I am here for you. I understand your needs and am committed to your care." Whether it's through your website, your office space, or the tone of your communication, everything you do should reflect your commitment to their well-being.

As patients move from first contact to first appointment, your brand continues to speak for you. From the moment someone visits your website to the moment they walk into your office, your brand is already making an impression. Every interaction counts. The tone of your emails, the design of your intake forms, the layout of your website, and the quality of your patient care all contribute to how your practice is perceived. Patients are not just evaluating your qualifications; they're evaluating your approachability, your professionalism, and whether they feel comfortable opening up to you.

Your brand should invite patients in, make them feel welcome, and reassure them that they're in the hands of someone who understands their concerns and will work with them to achieve their goals.

Consistency is key to building that trust. When your message and visual identity are consistent across all platforms, patients begin to feel confident and familiar with your practice. Whether they're reading a blog post, interacting with your social media, or walking through your office doors, your branding should feel cohesive. It should align with your values, your mission, and the type of care you offer.

Branding is not just marketing; it's about creating an experience. You are shaping how patients view you and your practice long before they even sit in your office.

A strong brand creates the foundation for growth. It builds a community of loyal patients who feel connected to your practice. When your brand speaks to the needs of your ideal patients and reflects your authentic self, it becomes easier to build lasting relationships and sustain long-term success. Branding is an investment—one that builds trust, attracts the right clients, and sets you apart in a crowded market.

So, take the time to build a brand that not only reflects your professional expertise but also your passion for patient care. When your brand connects emotionally with your patients, you create more than a practice; you create a place where people feel supported, cared for, and heard. You're more than a healthcare provider; you're a trusted partner in your patients' health journey. Let your brand reflect that, and watch your practice grow with authenticity, trust, and impact.

Define Your Brand Voice

As your brand identity becomes clearer, the next step is defining your brand voice—the tone, personality, and communication style you use across all platforms, from your website to social media to patient interactions. Your brand voice shapes how patients perceive you and how they connect with your message. It should align with the values and mission of your practice and resonate with the patients you most want to serve.

Here's how to define the tone that works best for you:

- Are you clinical and direct? If you value efficiency, clarity, and precision, a clinical and direct voice may be the best fit. This approach is ideal for patients who prefer straightforward, no-nonsense communication. It's about delivering information quickly and keeping the focus on the facts. Your voice is confident, professional, and communicates expertise without unnecessary fluff.
- Gentle and warm? If your approach centers on creating a safe space for healing, a gentle and warm voice may be more fitting. This tone is comforting, compassionate, and empathetic—ideal for patients who need to feel heard, understood, and supported. With a gentle voice, you convey care and reassurance, helping patients feel at ease in what can often be a stressful or uncertain environment.
- Spiritual and empowering? For providers who incorporate holistic, spiritual, or empowerment-based practices, a spiritual and empowering voice may be the strongest connection point with ideal patients. This voice is uplifting, motivational, and focused on growth, healing, and personal transformation. It encourages patients to take an active role in their health and empowers them to make positive changes. Your voice feels like a guide, supporting your patients' journeys toward wholeness.

It's important to remember that your brand voice doesn't need to be one-dimensional. Your voice can evolve as your practice grows or shift depending on the context—more formal during a first-time consultation and more relaxed in ongoing care. However, consistency is key. Patients learn to recognize you through your tone, and that familiarity builds trust.

No matter the voice you choose, ensure it reflects who you are as a provider and resonates with the patients you want to attract. Your voice is your practice's personality, so make sure it speaks directly to the heart of your patients, creating trust and emotional connection along the way.

Visual Exercise: Your Brand Voice Map

Pick 3 words that describe how you want your patients to feel (e.g., Calm, Clarity, Confidence). Let those guide everything.

Tone	Description	Patient Emotion
Calm	Steady, thoughtful	Safe
Bold	Strong, clear	Confident
Compassionate	Gentle, open	Understood

Choose Your Niche

As you clarify your voice, the next step is narrowing your focus. Choosing a niche is one of the most crucial decisions you'll make when building your practice. Your brand stands out when it's specific. When you focus on a particular area of care—such as eating disorders, PTSD, OCD, personality disorders, or trauma-informed care—you create an identity patients can immediately connect with. Specializing in a defined area helps you attract the right clients who are actively seeking your expertise.

Don't try to be everything to everyone. It can be tempting to take on all types of cases in an effort to grow quickly, but that approach often leaves you spread too thin and disconnected from your true mission. Instead, choose something that excites you, something you feel passionate about, and something you enjoy doing every day.

When you focus on a specific niche, your practice becomes a destination for the patients who need exactly what you offer. The more specific your focus, the easier it is to attract your ideal clients—those who resonate with your expertise and are more likely to trust and value your services. This clarity allows you to refine your skills in one area, becoming the go-to expert for those in need. Your reputation grows faster, your marketing becomes more effective, and your impact deepens.

You're far less likely to feel burnt out when working in an area you love. When you're passionate about your work, it doesn't feel like a chore; it feels like a calling. And when you bring that energy into your practice, patients feel it. They sense your commitment and expertise, and they're more inclined to engage with you for long-term care.

Ultimately, choosing a niche is what will set you apart. It makes your practice more memorable, easier to market, and easier to refer. The more specific you are, the easier it becomes for people to find you, trust you, and recommend you. Pick a niche that feels right for you and build your brand around it. Your niche is your superpower—use it to create the practice you've always dreamed of.

Why This Matters for Your Brand

As you refine your niche, it becomes equally important to understand the people you serve. Knowing what your patients are navigating allows your branding to land more powerfully and compassionately. Here is a comprehensive reference list of widely recognized DSM-5 disorders, alongside estimated prevalence rates among adults in the U.S.

Table: Common DSM-5 Disorders and Prevalence in the U.S.

DSM-5 Disorder	Estimated U.S. Prevalence
Adjustment Disorders	**5–20%**
Alcohol Use Disorder	**5.3%**
Anorexia Nervosa	**0.6%**
Antisocial Personality Disorder	**1.0%**
Attention-Deficit/Hyperactivity Disorder (ADHD)	**4.4%**
Avoidant Personality Disorder	**2.4%**
Binge-Eating Disorder	**1.2%**
Bipolar I and II Disorder	**2.8%**
Borderline Personality Disorder	**1.6%**

Conduct Disorder	**2–10%**
Dissociative Identity Disorder	**0.01–1.0%**
Generalized Anxiety Disorder	**3.1%**
Gender Dysphoria	**0.005–0.014%**
Insomnia Disorder	**6.2%**
Major Depressive Disorder	**7.1%**
Obsessive-Compulsive Disorder (OCD)	**1.2%**
Opioid Use Disorder	**0.8%**
Oppositional Defiant Disorder	**3.3%**
Panic Disorder	**2.7%**
Post-Traumatic Stress Disorder (PTSD)	**3.6%**
Schizophrenia Spectrum/Psychotic Disorders	**0.3%**
Social Anxiety Disorder	**7.1%**
Somatic Symptom Disorder	**5–7%**
Specific Phobias	**8.7%**
Substance Use Disorders (overall)	**7.4%**

Tip: This data can help you shape your copywriting, website navigation, and visibility campaigns around the most relevant struggles your audience faces. If your niche aligns with one or more of these conditions, name it boldly and compassionately in your materials.

Your Online Presence: First Impressions That Convert

In today's digital world, your online presence is often the first impression potential clients have of your practice. Whether they discover you on platforms like Psychology Today, Healthgrades, or through a simple Google search, it's essential that your online profiles speak directly to their needs and concerns. Your messaging must be clear, inviting, and trustworthy—resonating emotionally and converting curiosity into action.

Imagine your profile as your digital handshake. A strong online presence builds trust, demonstrates expertise, and shows potential patients you can support them on their journey.

Your message should feel authentic and speak directly to the emotions and challenges your potential clients face. Focus on:

- **Clarity**: Clearly articulate what you specialize in and who you serve.
- **Trust**: Provide credentials, testimonials, and a clear list of services.
- **Connection**: Share why you care about helping them and what drives your practice.

Being listed on online directories is crucial to optimize your profiles by keeping information accurate, using strong keywords, including testimonials, and highlighting specializations. Good reviews influence decisions—encourage satisfied clients to leave feedback.

Claim and optimize your Google My Business profile for local visibility. Use niche-related keywords in SEO to appear in relevant searches. Content (blogs, social posts, videos) builds credibility and gives prospects a sense of working with you before booking.

Consistency is key. Keep profiles and strategies updated and engage regularly. You are a trusted partner in your patients' journey—let your digital presence reflect that.

Optimize Your Psychology Today Profile

Your Psychology Today listing is a crucial touchpoint—your front door. Speak like a human, not a textbook.

Tips for a compelling profile:

- Use real, conversational language.
- Speak directly to your ideal client's emotional pain points.
- Include a warm, professional headshot (avoid casual selfies).

Pro Tip: Focus on transformation—what life feels like after working with you.

Example: Weak: "I am a therapist." Strong: "If anxiety is holding you back, I'm here to help you reclaim your calm."

Build a Website That Reflects You

Clients often visit your website before reaching out. It's where your story, specialties, and values come to life.

Platform options: SimplePractice (add-on), Squarespace or Wix, or Linktree for minimalist setups.

Must include:

- Services offered (therapy, evaluations, consultations, etc.)
- Fees, insurance, or cash-pay policies
- Concise, inviting bio in your brand voice
- Visible contact form or scheduling link

Suggested flow: Homepage → Services → About → FAQs → Contact

Your website should feel like a safe space—simple, welcoming, aligned with your ideal client's needs.

Expand Reach: Other Directories and Networks

- Zocdoc: Great for insurance; instant booking and availability filters.
- TherapyDen, GoodTherapy, Open Path Collective: Alternative audiences.
- Membership organizations: Check association directories (e.g., relevant medical/aesthetic groups).

Across platforms, maintain: focused bio highlighting your niche, credentials/licenses, scheduling links, and consistent photo + language.

Additional Visibility and Relationship Building

If scaling quickly, test Google Ads wisely (local niche keywords, modest budget, dedicated landing page)—but only after branding and site are clear/mobile-optimized.

Never overlook human connections: network with PCPs, counselors, other professionals; encourage referrals (HIPAA-compliant); create a one-sheet for partners with photo, specialties, contact.

The In-Person Experience

Small details matter. Offer bottled water (sparkling/still options), comfortable seating, calming colors/lighting, cleanliness, and thoughtful sensory touches to create reassurance.

From website to waiting room to follow-up, every interaction counts. A calm, professional, consistent experience eases patient anxiety.

Final Thought

Every platform—Psychology Today, Zocdoc, your website, or a referral—should feel like part of the same story. When your digital presence is clear, compelling, and emotionally aligned with your ideal client, your practice doesn't just get seen; it gets chosen.

Branding Isn't About Looking Impressive; It's About Being Relatable

When a patient finds your page and thinks, "They get me," that's brand success. Speak from your heart, and let your brand reflect the healer you truly are.

- Choose a Clear, Relatable Voice: Speak directly to your ideal clients, making them feel understood and valued. Ensure consistency and alignment with your mission.
- Focus on One Niche: Being known for something specific helps you connect deeply with those who need your expertise.
- Create Aligned Digital Assets: Ensure cohesion across profiles, websites, and communications.

Remember: trust is built with every word, image, and interaction. Consistency and authenticity are key.

You don't need to look like a corporation; you just need to look like yourself. Your authenticity is your strength. Be true to who you are, and the right patients will connect with you.

Chapter 5: Financial Mastery for Sustainable Growth

"You can't lead a mission-driven practice if you're constantly worried about money. Financial strength isn't selfish — it's foundational." —Dr. Daniela Rizzo

In private practice, financial clarity is more than just managing money—it's the backbone of your success. Too many clinicians treat financial planning as an afterthought, putting it off until they're fully booked or "busy." This mindset is a recipe for burnout and financial strain. Money is not something to worry about later; it's something to manage from day one. The health of your practice depends on it. Without a solid financial foundation, your dream practice could quickly become a burden that drains your energy and resources.

Here's the truth: you don't need to start big to make a big impact. Many new practice owners feel pressure to open a lavish office, hire multiple staff members, and decorate their space to "look the part." But unless you're a millionaire (lucky you!), this path can quickly lead to financial strain. It may look glamorous on paper, but starting with overhead costs you can't sustain can lead to disaster.

The key to financial success is taking small, manageable steps that align with your cash flow. It's tempting to believe you need a fancy office or a large team to succeed, but starting with what you can afford and scaling as you grow allows you to invest where it truly counts. There's no need to go all in on things that won't bring the return you hope for.

It's easy to get caught up in the excitement of opening your practice and feel the need to "look professional" right away. But overspending too early can break the bank or lead to a constant scramble to catch up. Remember: you're building a business to last, not to impress others. Think long-term. Prioritize essentials—like setting up financial systems, understanding cash flow, and budgeting for growth. Spend money on what helps you serve your patients better and streamline operations, not on superficial items that only look good temporarily.

Your financial systems will determine whether you burn out or create the freedom you've envisioned. When you have clear financial systems, you can track income, manage expenses, and understand profitability without constant worry. Financial clarity allows you to make strategic decisions about hiring staff, upgrading your office, or investing in marketing.

This clarity isn't just about numbers—it's about building a practice that supports your life goals. Being mindful of your spending ensures your practice is set up for success while giving you peace of mind to thrive.

The best advice for any new practice owner is to start wisely and scale with purpose. You don't need to have everything figured out immediately, but you do need a strategy. By avoiding overspending and focusing on strong financial systems from the beginning, you set yourself up for long-term sustainability. Your practice reflects your values, and financial stability is the foundation for a thriving business. Thoughtful investments, not flashy spending, will support your growth. Make your financial system your ally—it can guide you toward freedom, stability, and success.

For many clinicians, this advice lands deeply because of what it has already cost them to get here.

You've already made incredible sacrifices to get here. That student loan debt, sleepless nights, and relentless pursuit of knowledge have led you to this point. Now it's time to make decisions that sustain your practice and allow you to build the future you deserve. Start low. Go slow.

That mindset becomes especially important during the launch phase. When launching a practice, it's easy to get excited and jump into big investments—fancy office spaces, large staff, elaborate furniture. But rushing can set you up for financial stress. Starting slow doesn't mean failing—it means being strategic and laying a foundation for long-term success.

Here are practical strategies for starting wisely:

Rent Hourly or Use Coworking Spaces: Avoid long-term office leases at first. Rent space hourly or consider coworking spaces to keep overhead low while building your client base. As your practice grows, you can expand with confidence.

Use Telehealth if Overhead is Too Steep: If physical space is expensive or patient load is still growing, offer telehealth services. Telehealth expands your reach, adds flexibility, and reduces overhead. Many patients also appreciate the convenience.

Delay Furnishing a Physical Office: Don't rush to buy expensive furniture or set up a full office until your income is steady. Focus on what's essential—your practice, patients, and financial stability. Once revenue is consistent, reinvest in your space thoughtfully. This is a smarter, long-term approach than trying to impress with unnecessary luxuries upfront.

These choices may feel slow in the moment, but their payoff compounds over time.

Remember, success doesn't happen overnight. It's a journey, and patience lets you enjoy the growth process. Starting slow doesn't mean you're not ambitious—it means you're strategic, in control, and building a practice that lasts. By focusing on long-term goals and avoiding flashy, short-term fixes, you'll build a practice that not only survives but thrives.

Looking back, the difference between struggle and stability often comes down to early decisions. The hard work you've already put in will pay off as you make smart, sustainable choices every step of the way. Take your time, grow steadily, and you'll build a practice that is not only profitable but deeply fulfilling. Your future self will thank you for the wise choices you make today.

A neurologist opened a luxury office in year one and lost $50,000 by year two. A psychiatrist paid rent for a year before they had consistent clients, losing $25,000. Slow is strategic. Think of it like titrating medications or therapy goals—go steady, not desperate.

Use these questions as a final checkpoint before committing resources.

Ask Yourself:

- Is this expense directly helping me serve more clients or build stability?
- If my practice were paused for two months, would I still be okay?

Confidence isn't about spending—it's about sustainability. You're not behind; you're building smarter.

Real Story: Danielle, LCSW

"I used to say, 'My rate is $120, but I can reduce it if needed…' I was giving people an out before they even asked. Once I started owning my fee with confidence, I got fewer objections and more commitment."

One of the most effective ways to reduce administrative overhead and improve cash flow is through automated billing and payment processing. When patients can pay online, receive automated receipts, and have their payment information securely stored, the financial process becomes smoother for everyone involved.

However, automation should never replace human oversight. Regular review of your financial reports, payment processing, and accounts receivable is essential for maintaining the health of your practice. Set aside time weekly to review your financial dashboard and address any issues promptly.

Offering multiple payment options can also improve patient satisfaction and reduce barriers to care. Some patients prefer credit cards for convenience and rewards, while others choose bank transfers to avoid processing fees. Flexibility here keeps your practice accessible.

Efficient documentation systems are equally crucial for clinical and legal reasons. Your records should be thorough enough to support quality care and meet regulatory requirements, but efficient enough to avoid consuming excessive time or energy. Develop templates and shortcuts for common tasks—most EMRs allow you to create custom templates for different types of appointments, assessments, and treatment plans. Templates ensure consistency while reducing documentation time.

Regular backup of your data is essential. Develop a strategy that includes both automated cloud backups and periodic local backups. Test your system regularly to ensure you can restore data if needed.

Systems are not "set-and-forget" solutions—they require ongoing monitoring and refinement. Schedule regular reviews to identify bottlenecks, inefficiencies, or opportunities for improvement. What worked when you had ten patients per week may not work when you have thirty.

Seek feedback from patients about their experience with your systems. Are they finding it easy to schedule appointments? Are reminders sent in their preferred format? Are there areas where communication could be smoother? Staying informed about new technologies and tools can also benefit your practice, but adopt cautiously—let others work out the bugs before implementing major changes.

The goal is not just good individual systems, but systems that work well together. Your scheduling system should integrate with billing. Your EMR should connect with communication tools. Your backup system should cover all critical data. Map out your typical patient journey from first contact through treatment completion, and identify touchpoints where technology can make interactions smoother, more efficient, or more effective. Look for opportunities to eliminate redundant data entry, reduce manual tasks, and improve communication.

No one is coming to save you—but you were never meant to play small. Welcome to your new chapter. A thriving practice is not only clinically excellent—it's financially stable, predictable, and designed for longevity. You are not just a provider; you are the CFO of your vision.

Step 1: Know Your Numbers from Day One

Before opening your doors to patients, it's crucial to grasp your financial numbers. This isn't just about income—it's about understanding the costs of running your practice and structuring your schedule to hit financial goals. Ask yourself:

What are my monthly operating costs?

Include everything needed to keep your practice running smoothly—EMR systems, office rent, admin help, marketing, insurance, and any other expenses. Knowing these numbers prepares you for the financial commitment of practice ownership.

What is my target monthly income?

Determine how much you need or want to earn each month to feel financially secure and profitable. This goes beyond covering costs—it's about setting a realistic target aligned with your goals and lifestyle.

How many clients do I need to see (at my rate) to hit that target?

Do the math. For example, if your goal is $12,000 per month and your session rate is $200:

$12,000 ÷ $200 = 60 sessions per month

60 sessions ÷ 4 weeks = 15 sessions per week

Once you know this, structure your schedule to meet your goals. You might decide to see three clients per day, Monday through Friday, to reach your target.

Now that you know how many sessions you need, reverse-engineer your schedule to match these numbers. Start with financial goals, then build your patient load around them—don't create a schedule first and hope the income follows.

Knowing your numbers from the start gives you a clear vision of what's required to achieve your income goals. It helps you avoid the pitfall of overworking or undercharging without realizing it. With a financial plan in place, you can make smarter decisions about pricing your services, managing your client load, and structuring your practice to achieve consistent growth without the overwhelm.

Remember, you're not just a service provider—you're a business owner. Treat your practice with the same attention to financial detail that you give to patient care, and you'll set yourself up for sustainable success. Starting with clear financial goals and a plan to reach them ensures that you're not just working hard—you're working smart.

Step 2: Set Your Fees with Intention

Setting your fees isn't about pulling a number out of thin air or copying what others charge—it's a deliberate decision that directly impacts the financial health of your practice. When you set your fees with intention, you ensure your practice remains sustainable, profitable, and aligned with the value you bring to your patients.

Research Local and Virtual Market Rates

Begin by researching what others in your area—and virtual providers, if you're offering telehealth—charge. Look at rates per session and consider any additional services or specialty care that might affect pricing. You don't need to copy others, but benchmarks help you avoid over- or underpricing.

Factor in Your Specialty, Certifications, and Niche

If you have specialized training, certifications, or experience in a niche area, you deserve to charge more than general practitioners. Specialization adds value and expertise that patients need and are willing to pay for. Whether it's trauma-informed care, eating disorders, or advanced certifications, set fees that reflect your unique value.

Build in Profit Margins for Savings, Taxes, and Growth

Your fees should cover more than monthly operating costs—they also need to support future growth, savings, and taxes. Build profit margins that allow you to reinvest in your business and prepare for tax obligations. Planning ahead ensures financial stability and reduces stress.

Setting your fees too low can create a vicious cycle: overwork, underpayment, and burnout. If you find yourself seeing 25–30 clients per week just to cover costs, it's a red flag—either your fees are too low or your overhead is too high. Burnout is real, and if your schedule leaves you exhausted, it prevents you from providing your best care. Setting appropriate fees gives you the space and energy to thrive, not just survive.

Your fees aren't just about covering costs—they're about protecting your time and energy. Charge what you're worth so you don't feel like you're burning the candle at both ends. Balance is key to a healthy practice and a fulfilling life.

Setting fees with intention allows you to maintain control over your practice's direction, serve your patients more effectively, and invest in your own well-being and growth. Charge enough to make a living, grow your business, and maintain the balance you deserve. Your fees reflect your value and the care you provide—don't undervalue that.

You've worked hard to get here. Setting your fees is your opportunity to ensure your practice works for you, allowing you to continue providing high-quality care while thriving personally and professionally. Don't shortchange yourself—you're worth it.

Step 3: Build a Sustainable Payment Workflow

Creating a smooth and sustainable payment system is critical for maintaining the financial health of your practice. A well-structured workflow saves time and enhances the patient experience, making billing and payments seamless and professional. This system should allow you to accept payments easily, automate routine tasks, and track outstanding balances—so you can focus on delivering exceptional care without worrying about financial logistics.

Accept Credit Card and HSA Payments (Stripe, Square)

You need a payment processor that allows you to accept credit card and HSA (Health Savings Account) payments easily. Stripe and Square are excellent choices—they let you accept payments online, in person, and even through your website. Both provide secure, HIPAA-compliant transactions, essential for maintaining patient trust. Square also integrates with appointment scheduling and other tools, making it easy to manage payments alongside your calendar.

Offer Autopay for Recurring Clients

For clients with regular sessions or memberships, autopay is a game-changer. Platforms like Stripe, Square, or TheraBill allow recurring billing, ensuring you get paid on time without chasing monthly payments. This keeps cash flow consistent and reduces administrative headaches.

Send Automated Receipts and Invoices

Make billing transparent by automatically generating receipts and invoices. This keeps you organized while providing clients with clear documentation for their payments. Tools like SimplePractice and TheraBill handle automated receipts and invoices, saving time and ensuring timely, consistent communication.

Track Overdue Balances

Tracking overdue balances is a key part of financial workflow. You don't need to monitor each patient manually—tools like QuickBooks and Wave integrate with payment systems to send reminders or automated late fees. This keeps cash flow steady and reduces stress.

Sync with Your Accounting Software

A payment system that syncs with accounting software streamlines tracking income and expenses. QuickBooks and Wave automatically categorize payments, sync with bank accounts, and generate financial reports. This reduces tedious manual entries and lowers the risk of errors.

Recommended Tools

SimplePractice: Ideal for mental health professionals, it offers integrated billing, invoicing, and scheduling. Supports credit card and HSA payments, plus automated reminders. (User-friendly and my personal go-to.)

QuickBooks: Popular for accounting, integrates with several payment processors to track finances in one place, manage invoices, and monitor overdue balances.

Wave: Free accounting and invoicing software perfect for solo practitioners. Sends invoices, tracks payments, and syncs with bank accounts.

Thera Bill: Designed for therapy practices, with invoicing, billing, payment processing, and recurring billing features. Ideal for practices managing client payments and insurance.

Square: Integrates with websites, mobile devices, and POS systems. Offers scheduling features for managing appointments and payments in one place.

Stripe: Flexible platform that accepts credit card payments and integrates easily with other applications, ideal for telehealth and online appointments.

Zocdoc: Primarily a doctor-patient connection platform with payment integration. Allows patients to book and pay on the same platform. (Note: Some users report upfront fees that may be costly.)

A streamlined payment workflow is more than getting paid—it creates a predictable, stress-free financial environment for both you and your patients. By using the right tools for billing, invoicing, and payments, you save time, reduce administrative tasks, and focus on what matters most: your patients.

When your system runs behind the scenes—handling payments, reminders, and accounting—you build a foundation for growth. The less you worry about finances, the more energy you can devote to serving clients and building your practice.

Financial health is as important as clinical expertise. A well-organized, efficient payment system is a key part of building a sustainable, successful practice. By investing in these tools now, you create a workflow that supports your long-term success and well-being.

Step 4: Separate Personal and Business Finances

Create a dedicated business bank account and business credit/debit card.

Benefits:

- Clean financial records
- Simplified tax preparation
- Professional image

Pro Tip: Use QuickBooks Self-Employed, Wave, or Bench to track income and expenses. Link your bank accounts and let the software handle the heavy lifting.

Step 5: Plan for Taxes and Retirement Early

As a practice owner, you're responsible not only for patient care but also for the financial health of your business. Planning for taxes and retirement early is crucial for the longevity of your practice and your personal financial security. Many new business owners neglect this step, creating stress and financial risk later.

You didn't start your practice just to pay bills and survive—you started it to build a sustainable business that gives you freedom to care for your patients and plan for the future. By planning for taxes and retirement now, you ensure financial stability, allowing you to focus on what truly matters: your patients and the quality of care you provide.

Set Aside 30–40% of Income for Taxes, Retirement, and Reinvestment

As a business owner, taxes can take a significant portion of your income, so it's important to plan ahead. Set aside 30–40% of your income for taxes, retirement savings, and reinvestment into your practice. This buffer ensures you're prepared when tax season arrives and prevents scrambling for funds. It also provides a solid foundation for building wealth and growing your practice over the long term.

Make Quarterly Estimated Tax Payments (Q1, Q2, Q3, Q4)

Rather than waiting until the end of the year to pay taxes, make quarterly estimated payments to the IRS. These payments are based on your projected income for the year, so you avoid facing a large lump sum at year-end. Paying quarterly keeps you ahead of your tax obligations, reduces the risk of penalties, and provides peace of mind knowing your taxes are handled proactively.

Open a Solo 401k, SEP IRA, or Roth IRA to Build Wealth

One of the biggest advantages of owning your own practice is the ability to invest in your future. Retirement accounts like a Solo 401k, SEP IRA, or Roth IRA let you save while reducing taxable income. They give you more control over how your savings grow and offer significant tax advantages.

- **Solo 401k:** Ideal for solo practitioners, this account allows both employee and employer contributions, giving you the opportunity to save a substantial amount each year.
- **SEP IRA:** A Simplified Employee Pension (SEP) IRA is another strong option for solo business owners. It lets you contribute a large percentage of your income to a tax-deferred account, lowering your current taxable income.
- **Roth IRA:** With a Roth IRA, you contribute post-tax money, and withdrawals in retirement are tax-free. This can be beneficial if you expect to be in a higher tax bracket in the future.

Navigating taxes and retirement planning can feel complex, but you don't have to do it alone. Working with a bookkeeper or CPA experienced with solo practices—ideally someone familiar with therapists, coaches, or healthcare providers—can make a huge difference. A professional can help you:

- Set up an accounting system to track income, expenses, and deductions
- Maximize tax deductions and credits available to small business owners
- Optimize retirement contributions based on your needs and goals
- Advise on the best tax strategy as your practice grows

This guidance not only prevents tax-related headaches but ensures informed financial decisions that support long-term success.

Financial planning is about more than compliance—it's about creating a foundation for your future. The earlier you start, the more time your money has to grow. You're building a practice meant to last, so don't wait until you're overwhelmed to set these systems in place.

Remember: Planning today creates financial freedom tomorrow. By setting aside money for taxes, investing in retirement, and working with the right professionals, your practice becomes more than a business—it becomes a legacy. Build with confidence, knowing you're taking control of your financial future and protecting your personal and professional well-being.

Step 6: Upgrade Your Mindset About Money

It's time to get real: money is not just a transaction—it reflects your worth. Many clinicians feel uncomfortable setting prices or charging what they deserve because they don't want to appear greedy. But you're not being greedy—you're creating capacity. Charging appropriately for your expertise allows you to continue offering life-changing treatment and provide the best care to your patients.

You've worked hard to reach this point. Your years of training, professional development, specializations, and commitment deserve to be reflected in your pricing. When patients question your rates, remember that your price reflects the quality of care you provide—it's an investment in their well-being.

When a patient says, "So-and-so charges half," they're revealing a mindset that undervalues specialized care. You don't need to convince them. Simply explain that your specialty comes with years of training, professional memberships, and ongoing education. You're offering not just a service, but expertise and dedicated attention. If they don't see the value, they are not the right fit for your practice.

Your price reflects your value. You have put in the work to reach your level of expertise, and the care you offer is personalized to meet each patient's needs. You deserve to be compensated fairly, and the right patients will understand and appreciate your rates.

It's not just about money—it's about capacity. Charging what you're worth allows you to focus on delivering exceptional care. You can stay rested, resourced, and mentally sharp, rather than worrying about bills or stretching yourself thin. This ensures you can continue growing in your field and giving your patients the attention they need and deserve.

You want to help—but you can only do so effectively when you're in a sustainable position. If you're overworked, underpaid, or stretched too thin, no one benefits. Being able to show up fully requires being well-compensated.

Shift your mindset:

- "I feel bad charging this much." → "I'm offering life-changing care and deserve fair compensation."

- "I just want to help." → "I help best when I'm rested, resourced, and not worrying about bills."

Pricing is not just about paying the bills; it's about creating the freedom to continue doing the important work you're meant to do. You are worthy of charging what you're worth, and you are doing a disservice to your patients if you undercharge. When you raise your price to match your expertise and the quality of care you offer, you elevate the standard for your practice and the level of care patients can expect.

So, the next time a patient questions your rate, remember: you're not just charging for your time—you're charging for the expertise, dedication, and care you bring. Your price reflects the investment you've made in yourself and your practice, and it ensures that you can continue serving your patients at the highest level. You are worth it. Your patients are worth it. Charging appropriately is not greed—it creates the capacity to help more people and make a meaningful impact.

Dr. Natalie undercharged for her work and didn't separate her finances. After two years, she owed $18k in taxes and felt like quitting.

"I finally hired a virtual bookkeeper, raised my rate by $40, and set up auto-savings. Within six months, I was profitable—and proud of it."

Why Pricing Feels Hard

We're trained in service, not sales. Add to that:

- Cultural, gender, or identity-based money blocks
- Fear of losing clients
- Lack of clarity around value vs. time
- Attachment to acceptance and being "liked"

But pricing is not personal. It's a business decision that deserves strategic thinking and energetic alignment.

The Bare Minimum

Before anything else, you need to know your bare minimum to survive and operate.

Formula:

(Target Monthly Income + Monthly Expenses) ÷ Billable Hours Per Month = MVR

Let's break it down:

- **Target Monthly Income:** What you need to pay yourself
- **Expenses:** EMR, supervision, insurance, office, marketing, etc.
- **Billable Hours:** Realistically, 15–20/week (not 40) → 60–80 sessions/month

Example:

You need $7,000/month for salary + $2,000 expenses.

You see 65 clients/month.

→ Your minimum viable rate is **$140/session**. Anything less is unsustainable, no matter how kind your heart is.

Pricing Isn't Just About Numbers

It's also about:

- The confidence with which you quote your fee
- The alignment between your rate and your value
- The freedom your pricing structure creates (or destroys)

Your pricing either sustains you or erodes you. Choose sustainability.

Your Fee Models

Tip: If using a sliding scale, limit the number of slots and reassess quarterly.

- **Bottom:** Must-cover rate (bare minimum)
- **Middle:** Sustainable rate (ideal income + buffer)

- **Top:** Abundance rate (allows for reinvestment, scholarships, time off)

Sweet spot: Sustainable rate with strategic flexibility.

Sample Script:

"My fee is $500 per session. I accept payment via card and HSA. Let me know if you'd like to move forward with scheduling."

No justification. No apology. No overexplaining. You are not selling yourself—you are stating the investment for transformation.

Pricing + Value = Ethical Care

Charging too little doesn't help your clients. It can leave you feeling tired, stressed, and burned out. Fair pricing leads to:

- Clearer boundaries
- More energy for your work
- Better results for your clients

Boundaries to Implement:

- No-show, cancellation, and payment policies

Automation Tools:

- Stripe
- IvyPay
- SimplePractice Auto-Billing

Pricing Checklist & Action Steps

- Calculate your real cost per session using the formula above
- Write out your fee script and practice it 10x in the mirror
- Update your intake packet to reflect all financial policies clearly

- Choose one new pricing boundary to implement this week

When you price with clarity, you give your clients permission to value the work—and themselves.

Your Practice Needs a CFO (Yes, That's You for Now)

Until you grow enough to hire one, you are the Chief Financial Officer of your business. That doesn't mean becoming a spreadsheet guru overnight. It means you'll:

- Track what's coming in
- Control what's going out
- Make decisions that align with your vision, not your panic

"You can't heal people if your business is bleeding out."

Start by separating personal and business finances. Open a business checking account, pay yourself a salary, and get comfortable checking your numbers weekly.

Know Financial Snapshot: Your Numbers at a Glance

Before moving forward, let's briefly recap the core financial concepts introduced in Step 1.

- **Revenue:** All money coming into your practice — sessions, consultations, intensives, workshops, digital products, or other services.
- **Expenses:** All costs required to operate — rent, EMR systems, insurance, software subscriptions, administrative support, marketing, supplies, and professional fees.
- **Profit:** What remains after expenses are paid. This is your true business income — not total revenue, but what you actually keep.

Money Tip:

Use a free tool like Wave, QuickBooks Simple Start, or just a spreadsheet with columns: Date, Description, Income, Expense, Category. If you can track calories or patient symptoms, you can track dollars.

Budget Like a Boss

A budget isn't punishment—it's power. Start simple:

- 50% fixed expenses (rent, payroll, insurance)
- 30% growth/reinvestment (marketing, training, tech upgrades)
- 20% owner's pay and savings

Adjust based on your stage. Early months: reinvest more. As revenue grows, increase take-home.

"Budgeting isn't restriction. It's permission—to thrive."

Set Financial Goals That Feel Good

Don't settle for "enough to get by." Dream in numbers:

- How much do you want monthly? Yearly?
- What allows you to work 3.5 days/week?
- What would fund a team retreat or sabbatical?

Write it down, then reverse-engineer:

- How many sessions or packages at what price?
- Which are your high-margin services?

Profit First: A Gentle but Genius System

Mike Michalowicz's **Profit First** method flips the usual formula. Instead of:

Income – expenses = profit

You do:

Income – profit = expenses

Here's how it works:

1. Open **five bank accounts**: Income, Profit, Owner's Pay, Taxes, Operating Expenses.

2. Every time money comes in, divide it into those buckets. **Pay yourself first, not last.**

Why it works: It forces financial discipline and ensures you're not constantly operating in scarcity mode.

Taxes Without Tears

- Save **25–30% of all income** for taxes.
- Consider filing as an **S Corp** once you're making consistent profit.
- Hire a **tax professional who understands small medical businesses**—it's worth every penny.
- Keep good records. It's a form of self-care: it protects both your peace and your profits.

Money Mindset: Heal It, Then Build It

If you grew up with money shame, feast-or-famine cycles, or "money is evil" programming, it's time to rewrite that story.

"You are not selfish for wanting abundance. You are responsible for stewarding your impact."

Healing people doesn't mean you must suffer financially. Your services are valuable. Your expertise is rare. Your income **can—and should—reflect that.**

Money Systems = Freedom

Practical steps to create financial ease:

- Set a **weekly money date** (20 minutes to review finances)
- **Automate savings and taxes**
- **Review pricing every 6 months**
- **Celebrate milestones** (First $1K month? $10K? Toast it!)

Final Words

Financial systems are not about restriction; they are about freedom. When you understand your numbers, charge with intention, and automate what you can, your practice stops running you and starts supporting you. You don't have to implement everything at once, but you do need to take ownership of your financial foundation.

Money doesn't have to be boring. It's the oxygen of your practice. When you master it, not perfectly, but consistently, you create a practice and a life that breathe easier, feel steadier, and fuel the future you actually want. Mastering money isn't about greed; it's about growth, generosity, and grounding your dreams in reality.

Before moving on, choose one action from this chapter and implement it this week. Review your numbers, adjust your fees, set up autopay, or separate your business finances. Small, consistent steps create stability, and stability creates capacity.

Your fee model:

Model	Description	Pros	Cons
Standard Rate	A flat fee is charged uniformly to all clients	Simple and easy to understand	Offers limited flexibility
Sliding Scale	A reduced fee based on a client's income	Increases access to care	May become financially unsustainable
Packages	Prepaid bundles of sessions (e.g., 4 or 6 sessions)	Encourages commitment and upfront payment	Requires planning and effective marketing
Membership	A monthly retainer for continued service access	Generates consistent, recurring revenue	Not ideal for every type of practice

Chapter 6: Expansion Models That Work

"Scale with purpose, not pressure. Growth should serve your mission, not smother it." - Dr. Daniela Rizzo

As you develop streams of income and functional systems, it's natural to start thinking about the future. Once you reach stability, the question of growth arises—and the key is thoughtful, sustainable progress. Growth is exciting, but it must align with your values, lifestyle, and long-term vision.

However, don't rush into expansion unless you have solid cash flow and an operational foundation that can support the additional strain. Expanding too soon or too quickly can lead to financial pressure, burnout, and operational confusion. Strategic growth ensures your practice can handle added responsibilities without losing the focus and care your patients rely on.

In this chapter, you will learn how to evaluate whether your practice is truly ready for expansion and how to choose growth models that align with your values, lifestyle, and long-term vision. You'll gain clarity on when and how to grow, whether through hiring, adding services, creating programs, or building additional income streams, without sacrificing quality of care or personal well-being. This chapter will guide you in making intentional, financially sound expansion decisions so growth feels purposeful, sustainable, and supportive of the life you want to lead, rather than pressured or overwhelming.

Step 1: Assess Your Financial Health Before Expanding

To transition from reflection to action, begin by grounding your decisions in financial clarity. Before considering additional staff or expanding your physical office, take a deep dive into your practice's cash flow and overall financial health. Ask yourself:

- Can I comfortably afford expenses like salaries, benefits, or office space without jeopardizing current operations?
- Do I have enough reserves to manage unforeseen costs during expansion, such as marketing, new equipment, or training?

If you're struggling to meet monthly overhead, focus first on stabilizing your cash flow before investing further.

Step 2: Gradual Growth Is Key

Once your financial foundation is secure, it becomes easier to evaluate how—and when—to grow. While the temptation to expand quickly can be strong, gradual growth is often the most sustainable approach. Start with small steps that won't strain your existing systems. This might include adding one extra day of service, slightly expanding your hours, or slowly building your patient base before bringing on additional staff.

For example:

- Increase your patient load gradually, monitoring how it affects your schedule and well-being.
- Consider adding services like telehealth or group therapy before committing to more staff or larger office space.

Growing slowly gives you flexibility to adjust, refine your systems, and maintain consistent quality of care.

Step 3: Hiring Additional Help (When the Time Is Right)

One of the most common forms of expansion is hiring additional staff. This can help you manage an increased workload and allow you to focus on providing high-quality care. But hiring too soon may create overhead costs that exceed your income.

Here's how to think strategically about building a team:

- Hire when necessary: If you're seeing more patients than you can handle or feeling overwhelmed with administrative tasks, it may be time to hire.
- Consider bringing on an NP or PA: These providers can assist with patient care, freeing you to focus on higher-level tasks or services that grow your practice.
- Evaluate patient needs: Identify whether support is needed in intake, billing, or clinical care.

- Ensure financial readiness: Before hiring, confirm you can sustainably support salary and benefits and that the role truly contributes to growth.

You may also start by bringing on a part-time therapist, NP, or assistant to meet demand.

Benefits:

- Reduced wait times
- Administrative or specialty support
- Increased impact through a team-based approach

Decisions to Make:

- Identify necessary roles
- Post the position or recruit from your network
- Conduct interviews
- Create training documents
- Use shared EMR access and clear protocols

Step 4: Scaling Your Practice with Your Lifestyle in Mind

Growth should also align with your lifestyle and values. If you prioritize work-life balance, a large practice with multiple employees may not appeal to you. Growth doesn't always require expanding your physical footprint or team. You can increase your impact without increasing your practice size. Consider:

- Offering virtual services: Telehealth allows you to scale without additional physical space and reach more patients.

- Developing niche specialties: Focusing on a specific population or issue helps you stand out without needing more staff.

- Offering group programs or workshops: These allow you to serve more clients at once and increase revenue without additional one-on-one time.

Step 5: Avoid Burnout During Expansion

As you explore these options, remember to protect your own well-being. Just because your practice is growing doesn't mean you must overextend yourself. Maintaining boundaries, automating processes, and streamlining workflows supports sustainable growth.

For example:

- Automate routine tasks like scheduling, billing, and reminders.
- Consider hiring administrative support to reduce your workload.
- Take regular breaks, schedule vacations, and delegate responsibilities to maintain both professional performance and personal happiness.

Successful growth is balanced growth. Prioritize your well-being as you expand, and avoid decisions that compromise your quality of life or the care you provide.

Step 6: Grow with Confidence, Knowing Your Practice Is Ready

Once your practice is financially stable and your systems are streamlined, growth will begin to feel natural—and even exciting. Take your time, build with purpose, and expand only when the right opportunity arises. You've already put in the work to reach this point, and now you're in the driver's seat to decide what comes next.

The decision to expand should align with your long-term vision and the kind of life you want to lead. Be thoughtful, strategic, and intentional in your choices. Remember: success isn't about growing fast—it's about growing in the right way.

Final Thought:

You have the power to grow your practice on your terms. Expansion can be exciting and deeply rewarding, but staying rooted in what matters most—your well-being, your mission, and the impact you want to have—will guide you toward meaningful, sustainable progress. You're building more than a practice; you're building a legacy.

To bridge your lived experience with your broader mission, consider how your knowledge can serve others beyond traditional sessions. Your personal insights can become someone else's transformation.

Consider creating:

- A self-paced course on anxiety recovery
- A downloadable workbook for boundary-setting
- A parenting program for families healing from trauma

Tools to Explore:

- Teachable – Ideal for delivering self-paced online courses
- Kajabi – Great for bundled programs with built-in email marketing
- Thinkific – User-friendly platform with an intuitive course builder

Questions to Ask:

- Do I enjoy managing others?
- Is there demand for a broader set of services?
- Am I ready to become a visionary leader—not just a provider?

Important Reminders:

- Not all growth is good—protect your peace and your "why."
- Run the numbers. More offerings = more complexity (not always more income).
- Use systems to support expansion; don't sacrifice quality.
- Group therapy or coaching can expand your impact while creating community.

Examples:

- 8-week OCD Recovery Circle
- Monthly Trauma Healing Space for Professionals
- Virtual Postpartum Support Group

Logistics:

- Use HIPAA-compliant Zoom or an appropriate office space
- Limit group size to allow meaningful interaction
- Create a structured curriculum and provide prep materials

Bonus: Once your program is proven, you can license your group format to other providers.

Step 7: Building Beyond Your Practice: Expanding into Multiple Income Streams

As your practice continues to grow, you may feel called to build something larger—a brand that extends beyond the walls of your clinic. This shift often comes naturally once your foundation feels strong. It's not just about treating patients one-on-one; it's about expanding your influence and creating offerings that reflect your passions, expertise, and long-term goals.

If you're an MD, NP, or PA, there are many ways to diversify and build a legacy business that complements (or even enhances) your clinical work.

Launch an Aesthetic Practice or Med Spa

If aesthetics interests you, you can expand into cosmetic and wellness services. Pursuing board certification in aesthetics opens the door to offering treatments such as Botox, fillers, skin rejuvenation, and laser therapies. With the right training, you can even open a med spa—a model that blends beauty, wellness, and medical insight.

As a licensed healthcare provider, your medical background ensures these services are delivered safely and effectively. The aesthetic industry continues to grow, and clients actively seek professionals they trust. A med spa allows you to build a team, expand your brand, and establish multiple income streams within a thriving market.

Develop Mental Health Clinics or Specialized Practices

For mental health professionals, expansion can mean creating a clinic that goes beyond individual therapy. You might offer services such as psychoanalysis, individual and group therapy, or medication management. Bringing in clinicians who share your values builds a comprehensive center that meets your community's needs.

You can also create niche clinics focused on trauma-informed care, addiction treatment, ADHD, or family counseling. Specialization helps you scale while establishing your brand as a trusted resource in your area of expertise.

Write Books and Share Your Expertise

Writing allows you to reach people far beyond your practice. Books on mental health, wellness, therapeutic techniques, or self-help strategies can support both clients seeking guidance and professionals looking to grow. Publishing positions you as an authority and creates an additional income stream—while also serving as a powerful marketing tool for your practice.

Offer Retreats or Workshops

Retreats and workshops allow you to deliver deeper, more immersive experiences. Whether focused on mental health, personal development, or wellness, these events foster transformation in ways traditional therapy sometimes can't. You can also collaborate with experts in nutrition, fitness, or meditation to offer a holistic experience that strengthens community and connection.

Host Speaking Engagements or Mentorship Tracks

If you're passionate about education, speaking engagements, or mentorship programs, provide opportunities to share your expertise. You might speak at conferences, lead workshops, or host virtual trainings. Mentorship allows you to guide new professionals, share practical wisdom, and build a network that grows your influence.

Each of these paths offers a different way to expand your reach while honoring your mission. With a strong foundation in place, you're positioned to build something meaningful—something that creates impact far beyond the treatment room.

Offer Coaching Services

Another lucrative option for mental health professionals is offering coaching services. Unlike therapy—which is often clinical—coaching focuses on helping individuals achieve personal goals, overcome barriers, and enhance their quality of life. Whether you choose to coach on mental health recovery, stress management, or life balance, this is an excellent opportunity to diversify your offerings and reach clients who may not seek traditional therapy.

You can offer group coaching programs, one-on-one sessions, or online group formats to reach more people and support them in areas of life that extend beyond the therapy room.

Online Courses and Digital Products

Building an online course or digital product is a highly scalable way to share your expertise. Whether you create a course on managing anxiety, mastering stress-reduction techniques, or starting a private practice, online education allows you to deliver value at scale—on your clients' time and at their pace.

Digital products such as ebooks, guides, or audio programs offer another form of passive income, giving you the ability to earn while you continue focusing on your primary practice.

A Note on Intentional Growth

There is no limit to what you can build as a healthcare provider. Whether you're starting a med spa, opening a mental health clinic, writing a book, or hosting retreats, you can create multiple income streams that align with your passion and expertise. The key is to start small and scale in ways that feel authentic to you.

Remember, as a clinician you've already mastered skills like empathy, communication, and problem-solving—these strengths will support you as you build a second business and expand your influence. Build your legacy on your terms, and create a business that not only supports your income but also allows you to make a lasting impact. The world is waiting for what you have to offer—now it's time to take the next step.

You Are Allowed to Grow Beyond the Room You Started In

Don't ever let anyone tell you that you can't build your own business, that you're not capable of expanding your impact, or that you need to stay in a traditional job forever. This is your journey, and you're the only one who decides how far you can go. Yes, it may feel safe to stay in a hospital or clinic job—clocking in and out, following a predictable routine, and relying on a steady paycheck. If that's your choice, that's perfectly valid.

But for entrepreneurs like you, this book is your guide to something bigger—something with limitless potential. It's about building a business that reflects your vision, your values, and your ambition.

You have the power to create something beyond the walls of an office or the boundaries of a single job. You don't have to fit into a mold someone else designed. The world needs people who are willing to innovate, take risks, and create a ripple effect of positive change. This journey is designed for those who want to give back in multiple ways—through new ventures, meaningful products, or creative projects that expand what's possible.

Why Build Another Business?

You might ask yourself, *"Why build another business? Why not stay in a clinic job and enjoy the security?"* It's a good question. And if that path brings you joy, stay with it. There is no shame in choosing stability.

But for those who feel called to more—for those who want to create rather than simply follow—this book is for you. It's for clinicians who want to build something meaningful, sustainable, and impactful. It's for those who want to create multiple streams of income that align with their passions and benefit their communities.

Building another business doesn't mean abandoning your clinical role. It means expanding your influence, scaling your impact, and helping more people along the way. Whether through educational programs, digital products, or innovative services, your reach can grow far beyond the treatment room—transforming your life and the lives of others.

Intentional Growth, Not Just Impressive Growth

When you think about growth, remember this: growth isn't about impressing others—it's about being intentional with your next move. Every decision you make, every business idea you launch, and every person you hire should align with your purpose. It's not just about having a bigger practice or more clients. It's about creating meaningful growth that fuels your vision and supports your lifestyle.

Maybe it's launching a new service in your practice, creating an online course, or writing a book. Whatever direction you choose, make sure it reflects who you are, what you believe in, and what you want to offer the world. The most successful entrepreneurs understand that growth requires strategy, planning, and the willingness to take risks. But it also requires choosing opportunities that resonate with you—not simply following trends or doing what others think you *should* do.

Remember, you are allowed to grow beyond the room you started in. Your business can evolve into something that serves not only your clients but your life goals. Whether that means hiring a team to support your expansion, launching a new program that reaches a wider audience, or offering products that allow people to benefit from your expertise even when you're not in the office—the possibilities are endless. You don't need to stay small just because that's where you began. Your growth is yours to define.

Final Thoughts

So, what's next for you? As you grow your practice and move into new ventures, remember that you are creating a legacy. This is your opportunity to build something that not only brings financial success but also leaves a lasting impact on your community, your field, and the world at large.

Your next move should excite you—something that makes you feel alive and fulfilled.

"Don't ask what the world needs. Ask what makes you come alive, and go do it. Because what the world needs is people who have come alive." - Howard Thurman

Don't hold yourself back because you think you don't deserve to grow or fear that it will be too much to manage. You are capable of greatness, and the world needs what you have to offer. Whether it's launching a new product, expanding your clinic, or becoming a thought leader in your field, make your next step intentional and full of purpose.

You have already achieved so much in your career. Now it's time to take that momentum and expand your horizons. Let's build something extraordinary together—something profitable, purposeful, and deeply aligned with the life you want to live.

On my own journey, I can't count the number of times bosses, co-workers, and even friends told me, "Don't do it. Just stay at the hospital, inpatient, or in a clinic." And yes, it wasn't easy. There were nights when I stayed up working while my husband had to understand that there was a bigger picture. But I never gave up. I didn't let those doubts sway me.

To everyone who doubted me: I wish you well, and may the universe bless you. But I'm grateful I didn't listen. It wasn't easy—and I'm not saying it will be easy for you—but the rewards are worth the struggle. Today, I stand not only with a successful practice, but with a purpose-driven life, and I'm honored to share this journey with you.

You have everything it takes. You're ready to build your legacy.

Let's do this.

Chapter 7: Design the Life. Build the Practice.

"The first and greatest victory is to conquer yourself." – Plato

When I started my journey, I didn't just want to build a practice; I wanted to create a life — one that allowed me to control my time, make a real impact, and design something aligned with my values. I had worked for years in state hospitals, in multiple inpatient settings, and spent countless hours in the emergency room. Despite the long shifts and high patient volume, I didn't feel like I was truly helping. I began to ask, "What's my why?"

You didn't leave your W-2 job or finish years of training just to recreate the same chaos under your own name. You came into this field to make a real difference — to build a life that doesn't just sustain you, but fulfills you deeply.

That journey starts with intentional life design. When you shift your focus from merely running a practice to building a life that reflects who you truly are, you begin to attract not only the right patients but the right experiences, balance, and opportunities.

Freedom isn't about having more time off; it's about having the ability to control how you spend your time. Alignment means designing your practice around your passions and purpose. Legacy is what you leave behind — not just in your practice, but in the lives you touch, the boundaries you set, and the changes you make in your community.

This chapter is your blueprint for not just building a practice you run, but a life that energizes you, inspires you, and drives you forward. It's a chance to reclaim your time and shape your future on your terms. Don't just build a business; build the life you've always dreamed of — one that reflects your deepest passions and greatest potential.

It begins with the choices you make every day. In the pages that follow, we'll translate these ideals into practical steps you can take now.

Step 1: Define Success on Your Own Terms

Forget the noise — the Instagram metrics, social media, revenue targets, and flashy milestones that society often labels as "success." True success is personal, values-based, and, most importantly, peaceful. It's not about fitting into someone else's mold of what your career should look like. It's about aligning your professional life with your deepest values, your passions, and the legacy you want to leave.

Take a moment to reflect. Ask yourself: how can I help beyond writing a quick prescription and moving on to the next patient? How can I truly make a difference, rather than simply going through the motions of a demanding, high-pressure job? The work you do in your practice has the potential to change lives — but are you living your life fully in the process?

It's easy to get trapped in the cycle of doing what's expected: treating patients in and out, day after day, with little time to breathe, reflect, or rejuvenate. Real fulfillment doesn't come from merely "getting through" your day. It comes from aligning your work with your soul's purpose and designing your practice around the life you want to lead.

Reflect on this:

- What kind of day truly energizes me? Is it long, uninterrupted hours with patients, or the freedom to breathe between appointments? What type of work makes you feel most alive?
- How many clients per week is your ideal number? Not your maximum, but your ideal. Too many clients will burn you out; too few won't provide enough financial freedom. Somewhere in between is the sweet spot where you feel like you're helping while also honoring your well-being.
- What would my life look like if my practice truly served my well-being? Imagine waking up to a day when you don't feel rushed or overwhelmed — a day when you're energized by your patients and still have time to nurture passions and life outside the office.

Example:

"Success for me means working 3.5 days per week, taking every August off to recharge, and earning $150k+ while leading a trauma-focused group that brings real, impactful healing to my community."

This is your version of success — not someone else's. It's a chance to build a career and a life that supports you financially and nurtures your soul, energy, and peace of mind.

So ask yourself: What does success truly look like for you? How can you build a practice that doesn't just help others but helps you thrive too?

Take your time with these questions. This isn't a race. The answers will come when you're ready to step into your power. Create a life and a practice that reflect your deepest desires and biggest potential. You are worthy of that.

Step 2: Schedule by Energy, Not Just Time

We've been taught to schedule by the hour — to fill every block with appointments, tasks, and obligations. But real productivity and satisfaction come when we honor our energy rhythms rather than rigidly sticking to the clock. Each person has a natural ebb and flow throughout the day, and when you align your schedule with these rhythms, you can do your best work with less stress and more ease.

Before you shift into practical scheduling tools, it helps to connect this idea back to your personal story: building a life you love requires protecting the energy that fuels that life. Your schedule becomes not just a calendar, but a form of self-respect.

Think about your energy peaks. When do you feel most focused and creative? When do you feel mentally drained or in need of recovery? Honoring these natural shifts is essential to avoiding burnout and maintaining your passion for the work you do.

Consider:

When are you most energized?

Are you sharpest in the morning, or do you think best in the afternoon or evening? Schedule deep, focused work during your high-energy times.

When do you need breaks or rest?

Don't fill every moment of your day with tasks. Recognize when you need recovery time — and don't feel guilty about it. You can't serve your patients well if you're running on empty. Schedule recovery intentionally, whether it's a walk, a nap, or a few quiet minutes away from your desk.

When are you most creative?

Many people experience creativity spikes at predictable times of day. If you're developing new programs, creating content, or brainstorming, protect these creative windows.

Tools:

One effective strategy is using a color-coded calendar. This makes it easy to visually separate and balance tasks according to energy and focus:

- **Client Work:** Use one color for patient appointments.
- **Admin:** Another color for emails, billing, paperwork.
- **Creative Tasks:** A color for content creation, brainstorming, and program development.
- **Recovery/Personal Time:** A designated color for rest and self-care to ensure it's not forgotten.

Example:

- **No Clients on Fridays:** Dedicate Fridays to admin, deep thinking, or personal time.
- **Mondays = Light Half-Day:** Ease into the week with lighter appointments or small tasks.
- **Thursdays = Deep Work Only:** Reserve Thursdays for long-term projects, writing, or program creation. No meetings or admin tasks.

By aligning your schedule with your energy — instead of forcing your energy to fit the clock — your days begin to flow with more ease. Your work feels more fulfilling, and you can give your best to your patients and practice without draining yourself.

Remember: your time is valuable, but your energy is what allows you to excel. Honoring both sets the foundation for long-term success.

Step 3: Align Practice Structure with Lifestyle Goals

As you transition from managing your energy to shaping your practice, think of this as the next layer of life design. Protecting your energy is powerful — but structuring your practice to support the life you want is what makes the change sustainable.

Your practice should work for you, not the other way around. If you find that your practice is demanding too much time, draining your energy, or limiting your life outside of work, it's time to step back and reassess. A fulfilling life begins with a practice that genuinely supports your goals and values.

Ask yourself:

Is your current fee supporting your desired schedule?

Are you charging enough to afford the lifestyle you want? Your fee should reflect the value you provide and the life you're building. If it doesn't, it's time to reassess.

Do your services reflect your passions?

Are you offering work that excites you — like groups, coaching, intensives, or workshops — or are you stuck in a model that drains you? Your enthusiasm attracts the right patients and makes your work more fulfilling.

Do your boundaries support peace?

Are your workload and policies sustainable? If you consistently feel overwhelmed or if clients repeatedly push limits, your boundaries likely need strengthening. Clearer structures around no-shows, office hours, and client load protect both your well-being and your practice.

If your current structure isn't aligning with the life you want, consider:

Raise your rates

If you're working hard without seeing the financial return you need, raising your rates is a step toward valuing your time and expertise. Higher value often means fewer clients and more balance — without sacrificing income.

Reduce the number of sessions per day

If your patient load is leaving you exhausted, scale back. Fewer sessions per day often leads to better care, higher energy, and more room for your own life.

Shift your model

Instead of offering only traditional hourly sessions, explore options like packages, intensives, or half-days. These structures often allow you to work fewer hours while providing deeper value to patients — and they offer far more flexibility.

Your practice should be a tool that helps you build your dream life, not a source of stress or confinement. By aligning your practice with your lifestyle goals, you create a sustainable and fulfilling career that allows you to do what you love while maintaining peace, balance, and financial security.

Remember: you're not just building a business — you're building a life. And you have the power to design it with intention and clarity.

Step 4: You Now Have Everything You Need to Build a Private Practice

The first few chapters have provided you with the blueprint: the essential steps, the tools, and the systems you need to start and run your practice successfully. From understanding your numbers and setting up your legal foundation to developing the right financial and operational systems, you now have the core structure required to bring your vision to life.

But let me remind you — **your journey will be uniquely yours**. My path may not be the same as yours. I didn't have a clear map when I started; I had to build mine through trial and error, through long nights of doubt and perseverance. Your journey may come with its own challenges, but you've already laid the groundwork. The difference now is that *you* get to shape the direction of your practice and your life.

You are the creator of your future, and this is your time. With this blueprint in hand, you can build something that not only sustains you financially, but also brings fulfillment, joy, and balance into your life. This isn't just about creating a business — it's about creating a practice that reflects who you are, what you value, and the life you want to live.

The steps are clear. The foundation is set. Now, it's your turn to make it yours. Take a moment, reflect on your goals, and decide how you want to move forward. This is your opportunity to build something that aligns with your personal values and vision. **You are the one who defines what success looks like for you — now go out and create it.**

Below is a sample values-to-action table:

Takeaway:

Make your values measurable. Turn them into actions that shape your decisions, schedule, and service delivery.

Step 5: Revisit the Big Vision

Take a moment to imagine your life and practice three years from now. Use this vision as a guide for the decisions you make today.

Ask yourself:

- Where am I living?
- How many hours do I want to work each week?
- What kind of clients do I serve — and in what ways?
- What is my ideal income — and what are the sources it comes from?

Let this vision become your compass. Use it to align your goals, boundaries, and business strategies with the life you truly want to build.

Simple Exercise:

This exercise will help you align your schedule with the life and practice you truly want.

Step 1: Create Two Columns

- Column 1: How your current week looks
- Column 2: How your ideal week would look

Step 2: Reflect and Answer the Following Questions:

- What tasks or commitments need to be removed?
- What can be automated or delegated to free up your time?
- What meaningful activities or priorities need to be boldly added?

Use this exercise to intentionally shape your time around your values, energy, and goals — not just your obligations.

Don't wait for burnout to give yourself permission to say no.

Set intentional boundaries now — they are essential tools for designing a sustainable, fulfilling practice.

Start with these simple steps:

- Identify and commit to your non-negotiable days off
- Set up email autoresponders to protect your communication boundaries
- End client sessions on time, consistently
- Protect your peace — and don't feel the need to apologize for it

Strong boundaries aren't barriers; they're blueprints for a healthier practice and a better life.

Affirmations

Now that you're a business owner — an entrepreneur — it's time to step into your power. Your practice isn't just a job; it's your business, your creation, your vision. As the CEO of your life and your practice, you are in control. Speak these affirmations aloud or write them down daily to stay anchored in purpose, clarity, and confidence.

I deserve a practice that energizes me, not one that drains me.

Your time and energy are your most valuable assets. You are entitled to a practice that gives back to you — one that aligns with your well-being and aspirations. Don't settle for anything less than a practice that fuels your passion, creativity, and success.

My calendar is a reflection of my values and priorities.

As the CEO of your practice, your calendar is your most powerful tool. It should reflect the life you want to create — one where you honor your values both in and out of the office. Own your schedule, and make it work for you, not the other way around.

I lead both my life and my business with bold, intentional clarity.

You are not just managing a practice; you are leading it. Every decision should be intentional, clear, and rooted in your values. Step into your role as the leader you're meant to be, trusting your vision to guide you.

I don't have to be everything to everyone — I only need to show up fully as myself.

You are enough as you are. You don't need to fit into anyone else's mold. Success comes from showing up authentically, offering your unique skills, and serving the patients who need *you*. Trust that by being yourself, you will attract the people you're meant to help.

Use these affirmations to realign with your vision whenever self-doubt, pressure, or overwhelm creep in. You are no longer just a clinician — you are the CEO of your practice. Embrace this shift and lead your business with confidence, knowing that every step you take is building toward the life and practice you deserve.

You have the blueprint, you have the skills, and now you have the mindset to create something extraordinary. Keep moving forward with boldness and purpose.

Action Steps: Build the Practice That Reflects the Life You Deserve

Clarity doesn't come from overthinking — it comes from aligned action. These steps are designed to help you gently shift from reacting to your schedule to intentionally designing your life, one aligned choice at a time.

Define What Success Means to You

In your own words, write down what success looks and feels like for you — not what social media says, not what others expect. Include your ideal lifestyle, income goals, and the impact you want to make.

Example: "Success means working 3.5 days per week, taking August off, earning $150k+, and leading a group practice focused on trauma healing."

Audit Your Weekly Calendar for Energy Leaks

Look at your current weekly schedule. What's draining your energy? What feels rushed, heavy, or misaligned?

Circle or highlight areas that need adjustment — and consider what lights you up, not just what fills your time.

A natural transition here is to consider how these observations inform the boundaries you set moving forward.

Choose 3 Boundaries to Honor

Put Yourself First: You Need Healing Too

As the owner of your practice, it's easy to get caught up in the needs of your patients and the demands of your business. But here's the truth: you cannot pour from an empty cup. To be the best for your patients, you must first be the best for yourself. Healing begins with you.

You are the heartbeat of your practice. If you're constantly giving without replenishing your own energy, you risk burnout, exhaustion, and even resentment. Your well-being is just as important as the well-being of those you serve. Make self-care a priority, not an afterthought. Whether it's setting aside time for rest, nurturing your personal life, or allowing yourself moments of quiet reflection, tending to your own needs helps you show up fully for those you serve.

As you reflect on this, the next step is identifying the boundaries that will support your renewed intention to care for yourself.

Boundaries are not just rules; they are the blueprint for a sustainable practice. They protect your time, energy, and spirit — essential elements for long-term success.

Pick three small but meaningful boundaries to start implementing today:

1. **Block one day with no client sessions**

Give yourself permission to have a day dedicated to rest, reflection, or personal activities. This day isn't just about taking a break; it's about protecting your mental and emotional health so you can show up fully energized for the rest of the week. Honor your time just as you honor your patients' time.

2. **2. Turn on email autoresponders after hours**

Set clear expectations about when clients can expect to hear from you. You don't need to be available 24/7. By using autoresponders and maintaining business hours, you create space for yourself without the pressure to always be "on."

3. **End all sessions on time without apologizing**

Respect your time — and your patients' time — by ending sessions promptly. This isn't just about staying on schedule; it's about honoring your limits and setting healthy expectations for future interactions.

Boundaries Aren't Selfish — They Are Essential

Implementing boundaries is one of the most powerful ways to protect your well-being and your practice. It may feel uncomfortable at first, but it's a necessary step in creating a sustainable business. As you honor these boundaries, your practice becomes not only more manageable but more aligned with your values and purpose.

Remember: Your well-being directly impacts your ability to care for others. If you don't take care of yourself, you won't have the energy to care for your patients. Prioritize your boundaries, protect your time, and let these choices transform your practice and your life.

Envision Your Life and Practice 3 Years from Now

Close your eyes and imagine the life you want to be living. Where are you? How are you working? Who are you serving? Use the following categories to sketch or journal about your vision:

- **Lifestyle:** your daily rhythm, time off, freedom
- **Financial:** income level and sources

- **Fulfillment:** the impact you're making and how it feels

Once your vision is clear, the natural next step is to share it with someone who can hold it with you.

Share Your Vision with Someone Who Supports You

You Don't Have to Do This Alone

Building a practice is a monumental task, and the journey can often feel isolating. But you don't have to do this alone. Entrepreneurship isn't a solo endeavor, and no one expects you to carry the weight of your dreams by yourself. The road to success is made smoother through connection, support, and guidance from others who've walked similar paths.

As you consider your vision, inviting someone into the process can help anchor your commitment.

Choose One Person — A Coach, Trusted Colleague, or Mentor

The key to staying grounded, motivated, and on track is finding the right person to support you. Choose someone who believes in your vision, has experience in the areas you want to grow in, and can offer honest, constructive feedback. Whether it's a coach, a colleague who understands the demands of entrepreneurship, or a mentor who's been where you are, having the right support is invaluable.

Share Your 3-Year, 4-Year, and 10-Year Vision

Your 3-year vision is your roadmap for success. It encompasses your dreams, goals, and plan for how you want to grow and evolve both professionally and personally. But simply writing it down isn't enough — sharing it makes it real. When you share your vision with someone who will hold you accountable, cheer you on, and help you navigate inevitable challenges, you create a sense of commitment that pushes you to keep moving forward even when the road feels difficult.

This person doesn't just listen to your ideas — they reflect back the potential within you that you might not always see. There will be moments of doubt, frustration, or exhaustion, but a mentor or trusted colleague reminds you why you started in the first place. They show you that setbacks are often setups for comebacks, reflecting the possibilities and opportunities you may have forgotten.

Let Them Hold You Accountable and Cheer You On

The accountability of someone who believes in your vision can be transformative. When things get tough or overwhelming, their support reminds you to stay on course. They provide the extra boost of motivation you need to keep taking the actions necessary to build your dream, even on hard days.

Having this support is not a sign of weakness — it's a sign of strength. It takes courage to ask for help and wisdom to surround yourself with those who can guide you. You don't have to do this alone.

Choose that one person — a coach, trusted colleague, or mentor — who will support you, help you stay focused, and believe in your potential. With the right person in your corner, the journey toward your goals becomes smoother and more manageable. There is power in connection and community.

Final Words: Let Your Life Lead

Your Work Is Done — Now Enjoy the Life You've Always Dreamed Of, Helping People in a Meaningful Way

This chapter isn't about doing more. It's about doing what matters — with clarity, intention, and alignment. So often, we get caught up in the grind, trying to do everything and be everywhere. But real success doesn't come from endless to-do lists or burnout. It comes from aligning your work with your true purpose — building a practice that supports your life, not the other way around.

You are not building your life around your practice; you are building a practice that honors and enhances the life you want. This is the freedom entrepreneurship allows: the freedom to design a life aligned with your values, passions, and dreams. Your business is a tool — a vessel to make an impact and live intentionally. Your practice should be a powerful part of your life, but it is not your whole life. Your relationships, well-being, and personal aspirations come first.

You deserve a practice that serves you — one built around your vision, energy, and values. You are not here just to fill hours, hit revenue goals, or follow someone else's definition of success. Your practice is an extension of who you are and should reflect your best self.

Design your practice to support your personal and professional goals: your family time, creativity, passions, and personal growth. When your practice is built with your life in mind, it becomes something you love — a tool for impacting others and a vehicle for living the life you truly want. Not the other way around.

You don't need to be shackled to your practice, working long hours just to "make it work." You deserve a life filled with joy, peace, and space to thrive. The foundation is set; now it's time to enjoy the rewards of your hard work.

You have created something powerful. Now live the life you've always dreamed of — a life with time for yourself, for family, for adventure, and for everything that fuels your soul. You are not just helping patients; you are creating a legacy that honors your values and the incredible impact you have in the world.

This is your time. You've earned it. Now go live it.

Chapter 8: Launch: Your Complete Readiness System

"The only limit to our realization of tomorrow is our doubts of today. Don't wait for opportunities to come. Create them. And as you rise, help others rise with you." - Franklin D. Roosevelt

End of Book – Readiness Checklist

"You don't need more time. You need more focus." – Greg McKeown

Starting your private practice doesn't require a flawless blueprint or a perfect setup from the start. The belief that everything must be perfect before you launch is a common misconception. What truly matters is being prepared and clear about your mission.

You don't need a fancy office, a huge audience, or a 10-year business plan to begin. What you really need are three key elements to ensure your success:

- **Clarity:** Have a clear vision of why you're starting your practice. Define your goals, values, and the type of patients you want to serve. Clarity gives you direction and helps you stay on track when challenges arise. Once you know your "why," the "how" becomes much clearer.
- **Compliance:** Compliance isn't something to dread—it's a necessity. Understand and meet legal and regulatory requirements, including registering your business, maintaining proper medical records, and ensuring HIPAA compliance. Handling these properly allows you to focus on delivering the best care without fear of legal issues.
- **Structure:** Establish operational systems to ensure your practice runs smoothly. Set up financial systems, choose an EMR (Electronic Medical Records) system, define office hours, and create procedures to manage patient care efficiently. A well-structured practice allows you to provide consistent, high-quality care while avoiding burnout and unnecessary stress.

Launching your practice doesn't have to feel overwhelming. The focus here is on practical steps to help you set up your business efficiently, so you don't waste time or energy on distractions. The goal isn't to overcomplicate the process; it's to give you the tools you need to succeed. Avoid the temptation to perfect every detail before moving forward. As you build your practice, you'll learn and grow—and that's the real value of the journey. The goal is to take action, even if it's imperfect action. Every step, no matter how small, brings you closer to your goals.

Learning from experience and staying adaptable will make the process smoother and more fulfilling.

Key Points to Remember:

- **Perfectionism is a trap:** Many people get stuck waiting for things to be perfect before they start. The reality is that waiting for perfection only delays progress. Take action now, and adjust as you learn along the way.
- **Action is the key:** As you move forward with your practice, you'll encounter challenges and setbacks. The most important thing is to keep going. Every action, no matter how small, is a step in the right direction. Don't wait for everything to be perfect or for all the pieces to fall into place—just take that first step and keep moving.
- **Launching is a journey, not a destination:** Starting your practice is not a one-time event—it's a process that evolves over time. Your practice will grow and adapt as you gain experience and insight. Keep your focus on steady progress, and remember that every action, no matter how small, contributes to the bigger picture.
- **Clarity, compliance, and structure:** These three elements are essential for building a successful practice. With clarity about your goals, a commitment to compliance, and the right structure in place, you can create a practice that is sustainable, ethical, and fulfilling. These are the building blocks that will support you as your business grows.

Takeaway: Launching your practice isn't about perfection—it's about building a solid foundation and taking action. You're creating something meaningful: a practice that reflects your values and serves your community. Start now, and let the process unfold as you go. You already have everything you need to succeed—just take that first step!

The Private Practice Pyramid: From Idea to Income

Level	Focus
Foundation	Legal, structure, and compliance
Systems	Scheduling, EMR, billing, and communication
Visibility	Branding, referrals, web presence
Impact	Clinical excellence, outcomes, and expansion

Section 1: Legal & Structural Readiness

- Choose your business entity (LLC, S-Corp, or PLLC)
- Apply for an EIN (Employer Identification Number) via the IRS
- Open a separate business bank account
- Secure business licenses (if required in your state)
- Obtain malpractice insurance (specific to private practice)
- Confirm state licensure matches practice address
- Secure DEA registration (if prescribing)
- Draft your legal disclaimers, intake forms, and informed consent

Section 2: Financial Systems Setup

- Set your session fees and no-show policy
- Choose a payment processor (Stripe, Square, Ivy Pay)
- Plan for taxes: save 30–40% of gross income
- Choose accounting software (QuickBooks, Wave, or Bench)
- Decide on a retirement plan or savings method (Solo 401k, SEP IRA)
- Prepare a basic budget (rent, software, marketing, liability)

Pro Tip: Run a 90-day cash flow forecast—identify your essentials and determine when you need profit.

Section 3: Clinical Infrastructure

- Select your EMR (SimplePractice, Valant, Jane App, etc.)
- Customize documentation templates (SOAP, DAP)
- Upload HIPAA-compliant intake and consent forms
- Choose a telehealth platform (Zoom for Healthcare, Doxy.me, etc.)
- Establish session frequency and modality
- Design your patient journey (inquiry → graduation)
- Confirm backup and data encryption for records

Section 4: Brand & Visibility Audit

- Choose your practice name
- Secure your domain name and professional email (e.g., hello@yourpractice.com)
- Design your logo and color palette (Canva Pro or Fiverr)
- Set up a simple, mobile-responsive website
- Claim and optimize your Psychology Today profile
- Claim your Google My Business listing
- Draft your "Who I Serve" and "How I Work" statements

Section 5: Systems That Save Time

- Use a scheduling tool with automated reminders
- Set up a business texting or phone line (Spruce, Google Voice, etc.)
- Create an inbox plan (auto-responders, templates for common replies)
- Implement consent protocols for texting and email
- Establish procedures for cancellations, emergencies, and after-hours
- Optional: Hire a VA or assistant for administrative tasks

Section 6: Mindset & Mission Clarity

- Clearly define your WHY and embed it in your materials
- Confidently explain your niche
- Practice stating your fees without apologizing

- Identify who you don't serve—and know where to refer
- Define what "success" looks like for your first 90 days

Suggested Pre-Launch Timeline

Timeframe	Focus
90 Days Out	Legal setup, insurance, EMR selection
60 Days Out	Website, branding, profiles, and fee-setting
30 Days Out	Soft launch visibility (socials, referrals)
7 Days Out	System tests, boundary emails, and office prep
Launch Week	Start seeing clients — even just one.

Action Steps:

1. Print or copy this checklist and mark off completed items this week
2. Schedule your official "Launch Day" (even if it's a soft opening)
3. Share your progress with a mentor or peer to stay accountable
4. Choose 3 items to delegate, automate, or simplify
5. Track your wins — clarity breeds confidence

You've taken the first steps toward building the life and practice you deserve. The hard work, dedication, and vision you've invested now form the foundation of something incredible. Stay focused on your goals, keep refining your strategies, and never lose sight of why you started.

In the end, your practice is more than just a business—it's your legacy. It's your chance to heal, create, and make a lasting impact. The world needs more practitioners who care, who are committed, and who have the courage to build something that truly matters. You already have everything you need to succeed—now go out and make it happen.

Remember: You are the creator of your own future. Keep your vision clear, your values strong, and your heart full of purpose. Your journey has just begun.

Conclusion: Step Forward with Confidence

Years ago, this journey began with a tired clinician sitting at a desk late at night, staring at a screen filled with open tabs and unanswered questions. The search bar held more hope than clarity. The exhaustion was real. The desire for something different was even more real.

If you're reading this now, you are no longer that person.

You are no longer scrolling aimlessly, wondering whether it's possible. You are no longer piecing together scattered advice from blogs that assume resources you don't have. You are no longer asking, *"Can I actually do this?"*

You have a blueprint. What once felt abstract is now tangible. What once felt overwhelming is now structured. What once felt distant is now within reach.

But before you move forward, pause for a moment. Close your eyes and remember why you started reading this book in the first place. Maybe you were burned out. Maybe you were frustrated by broken systems. Maybe you felt undervalued, overextended, or quietly certain that your work could mean more if you had the freedom to shape it yourself. That version of you—the one searching late at night—deserves this moment.

This journey has never been only about opening a private practice. It has always been about reclaiming ownership of your professional life. It has been about sustainability, dignity, and alignment. It has been about building something that reflects your values instead of squeezing yourself into someone else's framework.

You are the architect now. Your practice will not just be a business entity filed with the state. It will be an ecosystem you design. The policies you write, the environment you create, the clients you serve, the boundaries you set—all of it will reflect your philosophy of care. You are creating a space where healing can happen without sacrificing yourself in the process.

Start where you are—but don't stay there. You do not need perfect confidence. You need committed action. Every successful practice once began as a messy first draft: a single office, a simple website, a first intake form that was revised ten times. Momentum is built through motion. Clarity is earned through implementation. The courage to begin will carry you farther than waiting to feel ready.

And as you build, protect your well-being fiercely. The whole reason you considered private practice may have been to escape burnout—not to recreate it under your own name. Freedom means nothing if you are exhausted inside it. Set boundaries early. Design your schedule intentionally. Price your services sustainably. Rest without guilt. A thriving clinician builds a thriving practice. Not the other way around.

Remember: this is your opportunity to make the kind of impact that once felt constrained. You are no longer limited by productivity quotas, rushed appointments, or systems that reduce care to numbers. You choose the depth. You choose the pace. You choose the population you serve. Whether you create access through telehealth, develop a specialized niche, or cultivate a practice known for exceptional, ethical care, you are expanding what is possible—not only for yourself, but for your clients.

Trust the process—but trust yourself even more. The checklists matter. The timelines matter. The legal steps matter. But the most powerful asset in this entire endeavor is you—your training, your integrity, your lived experience, your intuition in the therapy room. No consultant can replicate that. No template can replace that.

Comparison will tempt you. Don't let it derail you. Your practice does not need to look like anyone else's to be successful. It needs to look like yours. Authenticity is not a branding strategy—it is a sustainability strategy.

And when doubt resurfaces—and at some point it will—remember this: the fact that you made it to the end of this book says more about your readiness than any credential ever could. You would not have stayed if this wasn't aligned. You would not have read this far if the vision wasn't real.

So now, here is your call to action:

Stop researching. Start implementing.

Register the business name. Secure the domain. Schedule the consultation. Draft the intake form. Open the business bank account. Take one concrete step within the next 48 hours—no matter how small. Action transforms intention into reality.

You once sat at a desk wondering if this was possible. Now you are standing at the doorway of something you built with clarity and courage. Take a deep breath.

The system may have shaped your training—but you now get to shape your future.

Here's to the healers who refuse to stay stuck.

Here's to sustainable impact.

Here's to autonomy with integrity.

Your thriving practice is no longer an idea. It's waiting for you to begin.

Let's get to work.

Appendix A:

50-State Entity Formation Guide (PLLC/PC)

Each state has its own rules for forming a PLLC or PC. Below is a detailed checklist for each state, including links for Articles of Organization, Secretary of State registration, malpractice insurance, and EIN filing resources.

Alabama

- Entity Type: PLLC or PC
- Secretary of State: https://www.sos.alabama.gov/
- Articles of Organization: File online at Alabama Business Services
- Malpractice Insurance: HPSO, Berxi, CM&F
- Unique Step: Requires Certificate of Existence for license holders

Alaska

- Entity Type: PLLC or PC
- Secretary of State: https://www.commerce.alaska.gov/web/cbpl/
- Articles of Organization: Alaska Division of Corporations
- Malpractice Insurance: CM&F, HPSO

- Unique Step: The Professional license board must approve PLLC prior to filing

Arizona

- Entity Type: PLLC or PC
- Secretary of State: https://www.azcc.gov/
- Articles of Organization: File via AZCC eCorp
- Malpractice Insurance: Berxi, CM&F
- Unique Step: Must publish formation in a local paper (except in Maricopa/Pima County)

Arkansas

- Entity Type: PLLC or PC
- Secretary of State: https://www.sos.arkansas.gov/
- Articles of Organization: File at the Arkansas Corporation Filing
- Malpractice Insurance: HPSO, CM&F
- Unique Step: Requires a professional affidavit with filing

California

- Entity Type: PC only (PLLCs not allowed)
- Secretary of State: https://www.sos.ca.gov/
- Articles of Incorporation: Use Form ARTS-PC
- Malpractice Insurance: Berxi, CM&F
- Unique Step: Must obtain a certificate of registration from the relevant licensing board

Colorado

- Entity Type: PLLC preferred
- Secretary of State: https://www.sos.state.co.us
- Articles of Organization: File Online
- Malpractice Insurance: Berxi, CM&F
- Unique Step: Check with DORA for naming restrictions

Connecticut

- Entity Type: PLLC or PC
- Secretary of State: https://portal.ct.gov/SOTS
- Articles of Organization: Concord Business Services
- Malpractice Insurance: CM&F, HPSO
- Unique Step: Education board approval is often needed

Delaware

- Entity Type: PC preferred
- Secretary of State: https://corp.delaware.gov
- Articles of Incorporation: File Online
- Malpractice Insurance: Berxi, HPSO
- Unique Step: Annual report and franchise tax are mandatory

Florida

- Entity Type: PLLC or PA
- Secretary of State: https://dos.myflorida.com/sunbiz/
- Articles of Organization: Start Business Online
- Malpractice Insurance: CM&F, HPSO
- Unique Step: All members must be licensed in Florida

Georgia

- Entity Type: PC preferred, PLLC allowed
- Secretary of State: https://sos.ga.gov/
- Articles of Incorporation: eCorp Online Portal
- Malpractice Insurance: Berxi, HPSO
- Unique Step: Some professions are restricted to a PC structure

Hawaii

- Entity Type: PLLC or PC
- Secretary of State: https://cca.hawaii.gov/breg

- Articles of Organization: File with BREG
- Malpractice Insurance: CM&F, Berxi
- Unique Step: Must include professional license number with filing

Idaho

- Entity Type: PLLC preferred
- Secretary of State: https://sos.idaho.gov
- Articles of Organization: Idaho SOSBiz Portal
- Malpractice Insurance: HPSO, CM&F
- Unique Step: Annual report required and must include license verification

Illinois

- Entity Type: PLLC or PC
- Secretary of State: https://www.ilsos.gov
- Articles of Organization: Corporate LLC Portal
- Malpractice Insurance: Berxi, CM&F
- Unique Step: Use BCA 2.10 for PCs; must verify with licensing department

Indiana

- Entity Type: PC or PLLC
- Secretary of State: https://inbiz.in.gov
- Articles of Organization: INBiz Start Business
- Malpractice Insurance: CM&F, HPSO
- Unique Step: Must designate a registered agent

Iowa

- Entity Type: PC preferred
- Secretary of State: https://sos.iowa.gov
- Articles of Organization: Business Filings
- Malpractice Insurance: HPSO, Berxi
- Unique Step: May require licensing board review

Kansas

- Entity Type: PLLC or PC
- Secretary of State: https://sos.ks.gov
- Articles of Organization: Kansas Business Center
- Malpractice Insurance: Berxi, CM&F
- Unique Step: Naming must comply with the Kansas Healing Arts Board rules

Kentucky

- Entity Type: PC only
- Secretary of State: https://www.sos.ky.gov
- Articles of Incorporation: Kentucky One Stop
- Malpractice Insurance: CM&F, Berxi
- Unique Step: Submit a professional license with a business application

Louisiana

- Entity Type: PLLC or PC
- Secretary of State: https://www.sos.la.gov
- Articles of Organization: GeauxBiz Portal
- Malpractice Insurance: HPSO, CM&F
- Unique Step: Includes state tax registration in the setup

Maine

- Entity Type: PLLC or PC
- Secretary of State: https://www.maine.gov/sos
- Articles of Organization: Maine SOS Corporations
- Malpractice Insurance: CM&F, HPSO
- Unique Step: Use form MLLC-6 for PLLCs

Maryland

- Entity Type: PLLC or PC
- Secretary of State: https://egov.maryland.gov/businessexpress

- Articles of Organization: Maryland Business Express
- Malpractice Insurance: Berxi, CM&F
- Unique Step: Attach proof of professional license to the Articles

Massachusetts

- Entity Type: PC preferred
- Secretary of State: https://www.sec.state.ma.us
- Articles of Organization: MA Corporations Online Filing
- Malpractice Insurance: CM&F, HPSO
- Unique Step: Must use "P.C" in legal name

Michigan

- Entity Type: PLLC or PC
- Secretary of State: https://www.michigan.gov/sos
- Articles of Organization: LARA Business Filing
- Malpractice Insurance: HPSO, Berxi, CM&F
- Unique Step: Use "Professional Limited Liability Company" or "P.L.L.C." in name

Minnesota

- Entity Type: PLLC or PC
- Secretary of State: https://www.sos.state.mn.us
- Articles of Organization: Minnesota Business Services
- Malpractice Insurance: CM&F, HPSO
- Unique Step: File annual renewals online each year

Mississippi

- Entity Type: PLLC or PC
- Secretary of State: https://www.sos.ms.gov
- Articles of Organization: Mississippi Business Services
- Malpractice Insurance: Berxi, CM&F
- Unique Step: File form F0016 with initial registration

Missouri

- Entity Type: PLLC or PC
- Secretary of State: https://www.sos.mo.gov
- Articles of Organization: Missouri Corporations Online
- Malpractice Insurance: HPSO, CM&F
- UniqueStep: State-specific professional responsibility language required in filings

Montana

- Entity Type: PLLC or PC
- Secretary of State: https://sosmt.gov
- Articles of Organization: Montana SOS Business Portal
- Malpractice Insurance: CM&F, HPSO
- Unique Step: Must appoint a Montana-based registered agent

Nebraska

- Entity Type: PLLC or PC
- Secretary of State: https://sos.nebraska.gov
- Articles of Organization: Nebraska Corporate Filing
- Malpractice Insurance: Berxi, HPSO
- Unique Step: Professional affidavits required with application

Nevada

- Entity Type: PC preferred; PLLC accepted
- Secretary of State: https://www.nvsos.gov
- Articles of Incorporation: SilverFlume Nevada Business Portal
- Malpractice Insurance: HPSO, CM&F
- Unique Step: Must obtain a state business license in addition

New Hampshire

- Entity Type: PLLC or PC
- Secretary of State: https://sos.nh.gov

- Articles of Organization: NH QuickStart
- Malpractice Insurance: Berxi, CM&F
- Unique Step: Licensing board confirmation included with online filing

New Jersey

- Entity Type: PLLC or PC
- Secretary of State: https://www.nj.gov/njbusiness
- Articles of Organization: NJ Business Gateway
- Malpractice Insurance: HPSO, CM&F
- Unique Step: Must register with the NJ Division of Consumer Affairs

New Mexico

- Entity Type: PLLC or PC
- Secretary of State: https://www.sos.nm.gov
- Articles of Organization: New Mexico Business Portal
- Malpractice Insurance: CM&F, Berxi
- Unique Step: Include proof of licensure for all members

New York

- Entity Type: PLLC or PC
- Secretary of State: https://www.dos.ny.gov
- Articles of Organization: NY Business Express
- Malpractice Insurance: HPSO, CM&F
- Unique Step: Must obtain Education Department approval before formation

North Carolina

- Entity Type: PLLC or PA
- Secretary of State: https://www.sosnc.gov
- Articles of Organization: NC SOS Online Services
- Malpractice Insurance: Berxi, CM&F
- Unique Step: Certificate of registration required from the licensing board

North Dakota

- Entity Type: PC only
- Secretary of State: https://sos.nd.gov
- Articles of Incorporation: Business Registration Portal
- Malpractice Insurance: CM&F, HPSO
- Unique Step: Medical professionals must comply with the board statute language

Ohio

- Entity Type: PLLC or PC
- Secretary of State: https://www.ohiosos.gov
- Articles of Organization: Ohio Business Central
- Malpractice Insurance: Berxi, CM&F
- Unique Step: Articles must specifically identify the type of services

Oklahoma

- Entity Type: PLLC or PC
- Secretary of State: https://www.sos.ok.gov
- Articles of Organization: Oklahoma SOS Online
- Malpractice Insurance: HPSO, CM&F
- Unique Step: The Licensing board must verify status prior to approval

Oregon

- Entity Type: PLLC or PC
- Secretary of State: https://sos.oregon.gov
- Articles of Organization: Oregon Business Xpress
- Malpractice Insurance: CM&F, HPSO
- Unique Step: Check for industry-specific insurance thresholds

Pennsylvania

- Entity Type: PLLC or PC
- Secretary of State: https://www.dos.pa.gov

- Articles of Organization: PA Business One-Stop
- Malpractice Insurance: HPSO, Berxi
- Unique Step: Licensing board approval mandatory

Puerto Rico (it is an unincorporated territory of the USA- bonus)

- Entity Type: LLC or PC
- Secretary of State: https://rcp.estado.pr.gov/en
- Articles of Organization: File Certificate of Formation (LLC) or Incorporation (PC) via Puerto Rico Dept. of State Online Portal
- Malpractice Insurance: HPSO, CM&F (available for Puerto Rico-based providers)
- Unique Step: Must register in the Registry of Legal Entities in addition to entity formation; all filings must comply with Puerto Rico's General Corporations Act and local tax (SURI) registration required

Rhode Island

- Entity Type: PC preferred
- Secretary of State: https://www.sos.ri.gov
- Articles of Incorporation: Business Services Filing
- Malpractice Insurance: Berxi, CM&F
- Unique Step: Some licensed fields must submit a dual agency review

South Carolina

- Entity Type: PLLC or PC
- Secretary of State: https://sos.sc.gov
- Articles of Organization: South Carolina Business Entities
- Malpractice Insurance: CM&F, HPSO
- Unique Step: May require profession-specific state licensure ID

South Dakota

- Entity Type: PLLC or PC
- Secretary of State: https://sdsos.gov

- Articles of Organization: SD Secretary of State Business Center
- Malpractice Insurance: Berxi, CM&F
- Unique Step: All PLLC members must be licensed in the same field

Tennessee

- Entity Type: PLLC or PC
- Secretary of State: https://sos.tn.gov
- Articles of Organization: Tennessee Business Services
- Malpractice Insurance: HPSO, CM&F
- Unique Step: File corporate charter if PC selected

Texas

- Entity Type: PLLC or PC
- Secretary of State: https://www.sos.state.tx.us
- Articles of Organization: Texas SOS Direct
- Malpractice Insurance: Berxi, CM&F
- Unique Step: Use Form 203 (PC) or Form 206 (PLLC); require a licensing letter

Utah

- Entity Type: PLLC or PC
- Secretary of State: https://corporations.utah.gov
- Articles of Organization: Utah Business Registration
- Malpractice Insurance: HPSO, CM&F
- Unique Step: Name must reflect the professional nature of services

Vermont

- Entity Type: PLLC or PC
- Secretary of State: https://sos.vermont.gov
- Articles of Organization: VT Corporations Division
- Malpractice Insurance: CM&F, HPSO
- Unique Step: Requires a local business license in some counties

Virginia

- Entity Type: PLLC or PC
- Secretary of State: https://www.scc.virginia.gov
- Articles of Organization: SCC eFile Portal
- Malpractice Insurance: Berxi, CM&F
- Unique Step: File online with the SCC and professional board jointly

Washington

- Entity Type: PLLC or PC
- Secretary of State: https://www.sos.wa.gov
- Articles of Organization: WA Corporations and Charities Filing
- Malpractice Insurance: CM&F, HPSO
- Unique Step: File Professional Services Endorsement after registration

West Virginia

- Entity Type: PLLC or PC
- Secretary of State: https://sos.wv.gov
- Articles of Organization: WV One Stop Business Portal
- Malpractice Insurance: Berxi, CM&F
- Unique Step: Must get a business registration certificate

Wisconsin

- Entity Type: PLLC or SC (Service Corporation)
- Secretary of State: https://www.wdfi.org
- Articles of Organization: Wisconsin DFI Corporate Filing
- Malpractice Insurance: HPSO, CM&F
- Unique Step: Use SC designation in legal name for corporations

Wyoming

- Entity Type: PLLC or PC
- Secretary of State: https://sos.wyo.gov
- Articles of Organization: Wyoming Business Division
- Malpractice Insurance: CM&F, HPSO

Appendix B:

Several websites that therapists can visit for resources, tools, and support to help build and grow their private practice are following:

Psychology Today

- **Website:** https://www.psychologytoday.com
- **Purpose:** One of the most widely used platforms for mental health professionals to establish an online presence. It allows therapists, psychologists, and counselors to create a profile, advertise their services, and connect with potential clients.
- **Features:**
  - Therapist directory
  - Blog
  - Webinars
  - Resources for private practice marketing

Therapist Entrepreneurs

- **Website:** https://www.therapistentrepreneurs.com
- **Purpose:** Provides coaching, training, and community for mental health professionals who want to build a private practice.
- **Features:**
  - Free resources
  - Webinars
  - Coaching programs to help grow your practice

Good Therapy

- **Website:** https://www.goodtherapy.org
- **Purpose:** A membership-based directory for mental health professionals that helps them connect with clients. It offers resources on ethical marketing and practice-building strategies.
- **Features:**
  - Listing services
  - Professional resources
  - Training and events

Therapy Den

- **Website:** https://www.therapyden.com
- **Purpose:** An inclusive therapist directory focused on diversity, equity, and inclusion. It helps mental health professionals gain visibility and connect with clients seeking therapy.
- **Features:**
  - Therapist profiles
  - Support for marketing your practice
  - Network of professionals to connect with

Private Practice Starter

- **Website:** https://www.privatepracticestarter.com
- **Purpose:** A comprehensive guide and resource platform specifically designed for new therapists starting their own private practice.
- **Features:**
  - Templates
  - Checklists

- Free resources to navigate the business side of your practice

Therapists in Private Practice

- **Website:** https://www.therapistsinprivatepractice.com
- **Purpose:** Offers resources, courses, and networking opportunities for mental health professionals looking to open and grow their own private practice.
- **Features:**
  - Online courses
  - Free resources
  - Membership in a network of fellow therapists

The Center for Therapist Development

- **Website:** https://www.therapistdevelopmentcenter.com
- **Purpose:** Provides training and resources for therapists to develop and expand their private practices, focusing on business development, marketing, and practice management.
- **Features:**
  - Business training for mental health professionals
  - Marketing tips
  - Practice management tools

Therapy Business Academy

- **Website:** https://www.therapybusinessacademy.com
- **Purpose:** Offers coaching and online courses designed to help mental health professionals grow their private practice.
- **Features:**
  - Resources for practice-building

- Business systems
- Client acquisition strategies

American Psychological Association (APA) – Practice Resources

- **Website:** https://www.apa.org
- **Purpose:** A professional association for psychologists that provides resources for building and running a private practice, including legal, ethical, and financial guidance.
- **Features:**
  - Practice management tools
  - Marketing resources
  - Insurance information
  - Community support

The Private Practice Survival Guide

- **Website:** https://www.privatepracticesurvivalguide.com
- **Purpose:** Offers advice and resources specifically focused on helping therapists build and maintain a successful private practice.
- **Features:**
  - Articles
  - Webinars
  - Training on business development, marketing, and client management

The National Alliance on Mental Illness (NAMI) – Resources for Providers

- **Website:** https://www.nami.org
- **Purpose:** Provides mental health professionals with resources, advocacy tools, and information about legal and insurance-related matters that can affect private practices.

- **Features:**
  - Community-building opportunities
  - Insurance information
  - Advocacy support for mental health professionals

SimplePractice

- **Website:** https://www.simplepractice.com
- **Purpose:** Practice management software that helps mental health professionals streamline operations, covering scheduling, billing, and documentation all in one platform.
- **Features:**
  - HIPAA-compliant software
  - Customizable templates
  - Telehealth integration

TheraNest

- **Website:** https://www.theranest.com
- **Purpose:** A practice management system designed for mental health professionals, offering tools for scheduling, billing, note-taking, and therapy notes.
- **Features:**
  - Cloud-based service
  - Progress notes
  - Invoicing
  - Reporting tools

American Counseling Association (ACA) – Practice Resources

- **Website:** https://www.counseling.org

- **Purpose:** A professional association for counselors that provides resources for starting and growing a counseling practice, including ethical guidance, continuing education, and community events.
- **Features:**
  - Articles
  - Templates
  - Guidelines on building a private practice

Appendix C:

Following platforms offer resources, tools, and community support for various stages of establishing and growing a medical practice.

Medical Group Management Association (MGMA)

- **Website:** https://www.mgma.com
- **Purpose:** Offers resources for practice management, including business operations, financial management, and staff development.
- **Features:**
  - Online training
  - Templates
  - Networking opportunities
  - Industry best practices

The Private Practice Startup

- **Website:** https://www.theprivatepracticestartup.com
- **Purpose:** Provides tools, templates, and training for healthcare professionals looking to open and run a successful private practice.
- **Features:**
  - Business coaching
  - Client acquisition strategies
  - Practice management resources

SimplePractice

- **Website:** https://www.simplepractice.com

- **Purpose:** Practice management software designed to help medical providers with scheduling, billing, documentation, and telehealth services.
- **Features:**
    - HIPAA-compliant software
    - Patient portal
    - Customizable templates
    - Integrated telemedicine options

TheraNest

- **Website:** https://www.theranest.com
- **Purpose:** A practice management tool for healthcare professionals, including scheduling, billing, and documentation.
- **Features:**
    - Telehealth capabilities
    - Customizable templates
    - Easy-to-use scheduling tools

Medical Economics

- **Website:** https://www.medicaleconomics.com
- **Purpose:** Offers advice and resources on practice management, including financial planning, hiring, and marketing strategies.
- **Features:**
    - Articles
    - Webinars
    - Tools to help physicians grow and manage their practices effectively

The Physician's Practice

- **Website:** https://www.physicianspractice.com
- **Purpose:** A comprehensive resource for physicians looking to improve their business acumen and manage their private practice.
- **Features:**
  - Articles on legal, financial, and operational issues
  - Tools and resources for practice management

American Medical Association (AMA) – Private Practice Resources

- **Website:** https://www.ama-assn.org
- **Purpose:** Provides resources and tools to help physicians transition into private practice.
- **Features:**
  - Practice management guides
  - Financial planning resources
  - Information on healthcare regulations

Practice Fusion

- **Website:** https://www.practicefusion.com
- **Purpose:** An electronic health record (EHR) platform that helps doctors and healthcare providers manage their practices efficiently.
- **Features:**
  - EHR solutions
  - Appointment scheduling
  - Billing
  - Patient management tools

DocuSign

- **Website:** https://www.docusign.com
- **Purpose:** Facilitates electronic signatures for contracts, patient forms, and other legal documents needed in a medical practice.
- **Features:**
  - Secure document signing
  - Tracking
  - Management tools

Medical Business Academy

- **Website:** https://www.medicalbusinessacademy.com
- **Purpose:** Offers coaching and training specifically for physicians looking to run a successful private practice.
- **Features:**
  - Business strategy
  - Marketing techniques
  - Financial planning
  - Management tips for new practices

The Medical Practice Insider

- **Website:** https://www.medicalpracticeinsider.com
- **Purpose:** Provides information and resources on the operational side of a medical practice, including staffing, billing, and patient care management.
- **Features:**
  - Expert insights

- Case studies
- Resources for private practice growth

Healthgrades

- **Website:** https://www.healthgrades.com
- **Purpose:** A platform for healthcare professionals to manage their online reputation and connect with patients.
- **Features:**
  - Physician directory
  - Patient reviews
  - Profile management tools

Zocdoc

- **Website:** https://www.zocdoc.com
- **Purpose:** An online platform that allows patients to book appointments with healthcare providers, helping physicians gain visibility and attract new patients.
- **Features:**
  - Appointment scheduling
  - Online reviews
  - Practice management tools

Chamber of Commerce

- **Website:** https://www.chamberofcommerce.com
- **Purpose:** Helps local businesses, including medical practices, build relationships within their communities.

- **Features:**
  - Local networking opportunities
  - Marketing resources
  - Business listing services

Sonic Healthcare USA

- **Website:** https://www.sonichealthcareusa.com
- **Purpose:** A provider of diagnostic services that can support private practices with laboratory services and medical testing.
- **Features:**
  - Clinical laboratory services
  - Diagnostic tools
  - Partnerships for private medical practices

Appendix D:

This appendix guides Physician Assistants (PAs) through the process, providing tools, education, and support. It contains helpful resources for PAs to build a private practice:

American Academy of Physician Assistants (AAPA)

- **Website:** https://www.aapa.org
- **Purpose:** The national organization representing physician assistants, offering resources, webinars, and networking opportunities.
- **Features:**
  - Advocacy for PA practice rights
  - Business development resources
  - Networking and professional development opportunities

PA Foundation

- **Website:** https://pa-foundation.org
- **Purpose:** Provides funding, grants, and support for PAs pursuing professional goals, including starting their own practice.
- **Features:**
  - Leadership development
  - Grants for education and community health programs
  - Community engagement opportunities

Physician Assistant Business Owner (PABO)

- **Website:** https://www.pabo.com

- **Purpose:** A website designed for PAs who want to start and manage their own practice. Provides step-by-step guidance covering legal, financial, and business operations.
- **Features:**
  - Practice start-up guides
  - Sample forms, contracts, and templates
  - Advice on managing finances, staff, and operations

American Academy of Medical Practitioners (AAMP)

- **Website:** https://www.aamp.org
- **Purpose:** Offers tools for medical professionals, including PAs, to build or improve their private practice operations.
- **Features:**
  - Business management courses
  - Legal and financial resources
  - Networking opportunities

SimplePractice

- **Website:** https://www.simplepractice.com/
- **Purpose:** All-in-one practice management software for healthcare providers, including PAs. Helps manage scheduling, billing, documentation, and telehealth, especially useful for solo providers.
- **Features:**
  - Scheduling and billing tools
  - Telehealth features
  - HIPAA-compliant software for documentation and client communication

TheraNest

- **Website:** https://www.theranest.com/
- **Purpose:** Practice management software designed for mental health professionals, also useful for PAs in psychiatry or other specialties.
- **Features:**
  - Client scheduling and invoicing tools
  - Telemedicine integration
  - Secure record-keeping for compliance

Healthgrades

- **Website:** https://www.healthgrades.com
- **Purpose:** Allows you to establish a professional profile and be visible to potential patients. Great for marketing and building a new private practice.
- **Features:**
  - Online patient reviews and ratings
  - Profile management tools
  - Visibility and marketing opportunities

Zocdoc

- **Website:** https://www.zocdoc.com
- **Purpose:** Helps patients book appointments online and increases patient acquisition and visibility for your practice.
- **Features:**
  - Appointment booking system
  - Integration with other practice management systems

- Marketing support to attract new patients

National Commission on Certification of Physician Assistants (NCCPA)

- **Website:** https://www.nccpa.net
- **Purpose:** The NCCPA provides certification for PAs and offers resources helpful when considering a private practice.
- **Features:**
  - Certification and recertification resources
  - Job boards and career guidance
  - Continuing education opportunities

SCORE (Service Corps of Retired Executives)

- **Website:** https://www.score.org
- **Purpose:** Provides free mentoring and resources to new business owners, including PAs starting their own private practice. SCORE has a vast network of experienced business owners and experts ready to help.
- **Features:**
  - One-on-one mentoring
  - Workshops and webinars on entrepreneurship
  - Business plan templates and advice

QuickBooks Self-Employed

- **Website:** https://quickbooks.intuit.com/self-employed/
- **Purpose:** QuickBooks is a user-friendly tool for managing business finances, invoicing, and taxes, particularly useful for PAs running their own practices.
- **Features:**
  - Easy invoicing and tax tracking

- Expense management tools
- Tax estimates and filing support

Physician Assistant Forum

- **Website:** https://www.physicianassistantforum.com
- **Purpose:** An online community where PAs share advice, resources, and experiences about building and managing a private practice.
- **Features:**
  - Networking with other PAs
  - Business resources and discussions
  - Career development and private practice advice

The Private Practice Startup

- **Website:** https://www.theprivatepracticestartup.com
- **Purpose:** Offers step-by-step guidance and resources for PAs starting their own practice, including advice on marketing, business development, and practice management.
- **Features:**
  - Courses and webinars
  - Free resources and blog posts
  - Private practice coaching and consulting

Appendix E:

Helpful Resources for Nurse Practitioners (NPs) Building a Private Practice

1. American Association of Nurse Practitioners (AANP)

- **Website:** https://www.aanp.org
- **Purpose:** The largest professional association for nurse practitioners, providing continuing education, networking opportunities, and business-related resources for NPs starting their own practice.
- **Features:**
  - Educational resources and certifications
  - Business resources for NPs
  - Networking and advocacy

2. Nurse Practitioner Business Owner (NPBO)

- **Website:** https://www.npbo.org
- **Purpose:** Provides resources, guides, and coaching for NPs who want to start, grow, or scale their own practices, focusing on business development, marketing, and operations.
- **Features:**
  - Business planning and startup guides
  - Networking and mentorship
  - Webinars and coaching sessions

3. NP School

- **Website:** https://www.npschool.com

- **Purpose:** Offers comprehensive courses for NPs, including starting your own practice, private practice management, finance, and legal requirements.
- **Features:**
  - Educational courses for NPs
  - Business startup training
  - Legal and financial planning tips

4. Nurse Practitioners in Business (NPB)

- **Website:** https://www.np-business.org
- **Purpose:** Provides educational resources, workshops, and conferences to help NPs launch and manage a successful business.
- **Features:**
  - Workshops and webinars for business owners
  - Networking with fellow NPs
  - Business management resources

5. Private Practice Startup

- **Website:** https://www.theprivatepracticestartup.com
- **Purpose:** Offers courses and coaching for healthcare providers, including NPs, covering marketing, financial planning, and legal requirements.
- **Features:**
  - Step-by-step business startup guides
  - Coaching services
  - Resource-filled blog and free webinars

6. The Nurse Practitioner Group

- **Website:** https://www.npgroup.com
- **Purpose:** Offers resources and services tailored for NPs interested in entrepreneurship, including legal and business advice, and tools to start and expand a practice.
- **Features:**
  - Legal and business advice
  - Articles and tools for private practice growth
  - Client and marketing strategies

7. SimplePractice

- **Website:** https://www.simplepractice.com
- **Purpose:** A comprehensive platform for running a private practice, including scheduling, billing, telehealth, and client management tools. Widely used by NPs.
- **Features:**
  - All-in-one practice management software
  - Telehealth and billing integration
  - HIPAA-compliant document storage

8. TheraNest

- **Website:** https://www.theranest.com
- **Purpose:** A popular practice management tool for healthcare providers, including NPs, offering scheduling, billing, and charting features.
- **Features:**
  - Scheduling and billing tools
  - Telehealth capabilities

- HIPAA-compliant patient data management

9. Zocdoc

- **Website:** https://www.zocdoc.com
- **Purpose:** Helps healthcare providers, including NPs, list services, gain visibility, and allow patients to book appointments online.
- **Features:**
  - Appointment booking system
  - Online profile management
  - Patient reviews and visibility

10. TherapyRoute.com

- **Website:** https://www.therapyroute.com
- **Purpose:** A listing site for therapists, counselors, and NPs in the mental health space. Helps practitioners gain exposure to potential patients.
- **Features:**
  - Online directory for therapy and mental health professionals
  - Customizable profiles
  - Patient lead generation

11. National Nurse Practitioner Entrepreneur Network (NNPEN)

- **Website:** https://nnpen.com
- **Purpose:** A community and resource hub for NPs who want to become business owners, offering webinars, workshops, and networking opportunities.

- **Features:**
  - Networking with other NP entrepreneurs
  - Webinars and workshops
  - Online community and support

Finding low-cost labor lawyers can be challenging, as rates vary depending on the state, case complexity, and the lawyer's experience. However, here is a list of resources and strategies to find affordable labor lawyers across the U.S.:

1. Legal Aid Societies

- **Purpose:** Many states have legal aid organizations that offer free or low-cost services for individuals facing financial difficulties. They often provide assistance for employment-related issues.
- **Examples:** Legal Aid Society in New York, Los Angeles Legal Aid in California, and similar organizations in every state.

2. State Bar Associations

- **Purpose:** Every state has a bar association that often maintains a lawyer referral service. Many offer free consultations or reduced rates for those with limited financial means.
- **Examples:**
  - New York State Bar Association: NYSBA Lawyer Referral
  - California State Bar: Find a Lawyer
  - Florida Bar: Lawyer Referral

3. Legal Match

- **Website:** www.legalmatch.com
- **Purpose:** Connects people with qualified lawyers in their area. Submit a legal inquiry, and lawyers provide quotes based on the case specifics. Legal Match matches you with labor lawyers who offer competitive pricing.

4. Avvo

- **Website:** www.avvo.com
- **Purpose:** An online legal services marketplace that lists labor lawyers, offering reviews, ratings, and contact information. Many lawyers offer free initial consultations or low rates.

5. Rocket Lawyer

- **Website:** www.rocketlawyer.com
- **Purpose:** Provides low-cost legal consultations, document services, and lawyer consultations for employment issues. Offers monthly memberships and pay-per-use options.

6. UpCounsel

- **Website:** www.upcounsel.com
- **Purpose:** Connects businesses and individuals with lawyers, including labor lawyers, who charge affordable rates. Ideal for smaller businesses or individuals needing straightforward legal advice.

7. LawHelp.org

- **Website:** www.lawhelp.org
- **Purpose:** Helps low-income individuals find free or low-cost legal assistance. Offers state-specific pages to locate local labor lawyers who provide reduced fees or free consultations.

About the Author

Dr. Daniela Rizzo, M.D. is a board-certified psychiatrist and founder of a thriving private practice in New York City. But her path to building a successful practice wasn't straightforward, and that's exactly why she wrote this book.

After years of practicing emergency medicine and working internationally in Brazil, Dr. Rizzo faced a challenge familiar to many physicians: how to translate medical expertise into a sustainable, independent practice. She navigated the maze of business formation, licensing, insurance credentialing, and financial systems, often learning the hard way what worked and what didn't.

What sets Dr. Rizzo apart is her integrative approach to medicine. She combines conventional psychiatric treatment with nutritional medicine and regenerative health approaches, drawing on her diverse background to offer patients comprehensive care. This same holistic thinking informs her approach to building a practice: you can't separate clinical excellence from business sustainability.

Her personal experience with ADHD during medical licensing gave her unique insight into managing a practice while navigating the very real challenges that affect many healthcare providers. She's also witnessed firsthand how powerful nutritional interventions can be; her husband reversed his high blood pressure through dietary changes alone, experiences that reinforced her commitment to integrative medicine.

Today, Dr. Rizzo maintains a successful private practice in Manhattan, where she specializes in psychiatry, procedural medicine, aesthetics, and regenerative medicine. She is affiliated with Mount Sinai Health System and is a professional member of ASPARD, the American Psychiatric Association, A4medicine anti-aging, and AmSPA.

Beyond her clinical work, Dr. Rizzo is passionate about helping other mental health professionals build practices that sustain them financially while allowing them to provide the care they know their patients deserve. *The Thriving Practice* is the guide she wishes she'd had when she started her own journey from employed physician to practice owner.

Dr. Daniela T. Rizzo, M.D., PLLC

Psychiatry, Procedural Medicine, Aesthetics, Regenerative Medicine

100 Park Avenue, New York, NY 10017

Phone: 917-971-6757 | 516-447-3258

Email: info@drdanielarizzomd.com

LinkedIn: linkedin.com/in/daniela-teixeira-rizzo-2997361b1
Website: www.drdanielarizzomd.com

Affiliated with Mount Sinai Health System

ASPARD Professional Member and Mentor, A4M Member and Fellowship Candidate in Anti-Aging, Metabolic, and Functional Medicine, American Psychiatric Association Member, American Medical Association (AMA) Member, American Psychological Association Affiliate

www.ingramcontent.com/pod-product-compliance
Lightning Source LLC
LaVergne TN
LVHW090612110826
845146LV00001B/351

* 9 7 9 8 9 9 5 4 1 7 9 0 3 *